HIGH STAKES

Amy was standing in the hallway wrapped in a blanket . . .

Mike opened the door quickly and drew her inside. As he took her arm he noticed that her whole body was trembling. He led her over to the couch and splashed a shot of bourbon into a glass. He knew the symptoms. Amy was in shock.

"Drink this, Amy. Don't try to talk."

Her hands were shaking so hard she couldn't hold the glass. Mike helped her lift it to her lips. She coughed as the strong liquor burned her throat, then threw her arms around Mike's neck and sobbed.

"Hey, it's all right. Come on, Amy. Don't cry."

The blanket slipped down to her waist and Mike saw that she was wearing nothing but a thin silk nightgown. All the desires he had suppressed surfaced with a vengeance. How delicious it would be to comfort her with a kiss that would lead to much more. Resolutely, Mike pushed the thought back. Amy was in trouble . . .

Books in the HAROLD ROBBINS PRESENTS™ Series and available from New English Library:

BLUE SKY by Sam Stewart
AT THE TOP by Michael Donovan
THE WHITE KNIGHT by Carl F. Furst

Harold Robbins Presents:

High Stakes

A Novel by

John Fischer

NEW ENGLISH LIBRARY
Hodder and Stoughton

First published in 1986 in the United States of America by Pocket Books

NEL Paperback edition 1987

British Library C.I.P.

Fischer, John
High stakes: a novel.—(Harold Robbins presents).
I. Title
813'.54[F]   PS3556.I762

ISBN 0-450-41104-4

The characters and situations in this book are entirely imaginary and bear no relation to any real person or actual happening

Printed and bound in Great Britain for Hodder and Stoughton Paperbacks, a division of Hodder and Stoughton Ltd., Mill Road, Dunton Green, Sevenoaks, Kent (Editorial Office: 47 Bedford Square, London, WC1 3DP) by Richard Clay Ltd., Bungay, Suffolk

This book is dedicated to
RUEL AND JOANNE,
without whom it would
never have been written.

MENE, MENE, TEKEL, UPHARSIN . . .

*You have been weighed on the scales
and found wanting.*

THE BOOK OF DANIEL 5:25

Prologue

April 20, 1939

IT WAS A blustery spring afternoon. Gulls wheeled across a leaden gray sky, dipping and swooping in the cold wind coming off the Atlantic. Nicholas Spiros turned up the collar of his hand-tailored wool coat and shivered slightly. The white-capped waves breaking against the pier sent up a fine spray that drenched anyone foolhardy enough to get too close. Nicholas and his partner, Claudio Petrelli, were standing toward the back of the crowd, waiting for the passengers from the *Helena* to disembark.

Claudio watched as Nicholas glanced at his watch for the fifth time in as many minutes. "Relax, it shouldn't be long now. She knows you're going to meet her, doesn't she?"

Nicholas frowned and his eyebrows almost met over the bridge of his nose. "Of course she knows. My father promised her I'd be here." The wind had whipped Nicholas's black hair into an endearing tousle and he looked very much like a grumpy teenager, even though he was twenty-six years old, the same age as Claudio.

"Look, Nicholas, I've been thinking." Claudio stepped closer and waited for the clanging of the ship's bell to subside. "We have arranged marriages in Sicily, too. It's an easy way of combining land and wealth—that's why the tradition survives. Reluctant bridegrooms don't."

"We're not *that* barbaric in Greece." Nicholas winced. He certainly didn't want trouble with his intended wife's family. According to his father, she had three older brothers who were planning to come to America soon. "Once she gets here, we'll just have to make some sort of an arrangement. Like I told you, I'll find a way to send her back without insulting either family. I'll be as careful as walking on eggs."

Claudio smiled. Nicholas had made quite a hobby of collecting American expressions. "Maybe you won't want to send her back. There are times when our fathers are much wiser than we think."

Nicholas's dark eyes turned even blacker as he shook his head. "That's impossible. My father hasn't seen me in six years and he has no understanding of life here in America. I know exactly the kind of bride he's sent me, Claudio. Davonna Pappoulis is twenty-three years old. That's practically a . . . what's the phrase they use here?"

"An old maid?"

"That's it. Davonna Pappoulis is an old maid, especially in a country where most girls are married at sixteen. She's practically over the hill." Nicholas sighed and glanced at his watch again. He wanted to be back at the office, cataloging the new items that had arrived in yesterday's shipment. Claudio's father had added Italian lace to their line and Nicholas was eager to distribute it to the several large stores that had expressed interest. Then there were the usual tins of imported food and the icons from Greece. Despite the depression it was impossible to bring in goods from Greece and Italy fast enough to meet the demand from immigrants who wanted things from the old country, and they certainly couldn't keep the business running smoothly if they spent the whole afternoon at the docks.

The huge ocean liner sat heavy and solid in its berth as passengers milled about on the three high decks, eager to disembark after their long journey. A small boy started to climb the rail, but a buxom dark-haired woman grabbed him by the arm and pulled him back. For all Nicholas knew that woman could be Davonna. Nicholas could imagine her now, overweight, on the homely side, and pathetically grateful for the chance to come to America to wed a successful immigrant. She wouldn't know a word of English. Education wasn't considered important in a Greek girl's life, and Davonna Pappoulis had probably never read a book in her life. Nicholas was sure his father had chosen a nice girl who would keep an orderly house, but she'd be about as interesting as a loyal dog.

"Here they come!" Claudio grabbed Nicholas's sleeve and pointed at the gangplank. Nicholas nodded and pushed his way to the front of the crowd. He might as well get this over with. Davonna was sure to be terrified in this new land and he was determined to be kind and sympathetic. She wouldn't be here for long and the least he could do was to make sure she had pleasant memories of her brief visit to America.

"Nicholas Spiros?" There was a tap on his shoulder and Nicholas whirled around to face a small, dark-haired woman carrying a leather suitcase. Her cheeks were flushed and her eyes sparkled with excitement. She was pretty, extremely pretty, and even in the bulky coat she wore, Nicholas could see that she wasn't a bit overweight.

"I'm Davonna Pappoulis." She held out her hand and Nicholas took it automatically. "I recognized you from the photograph your father sent me. And this must be your partner, Claudio. I'm very glad to meet you both."

Nicholas stared hard at the pretty young woman. Her English was perfect, although heavily accented, and for a moment he was too shocked to say anything. Then he realized he was still holding her hand. "Oh, excuse me, Miss Pappoulis. I . . . I assumed you wouldn't speak English."

Davonna laughed, showing even white teeth. "Of course I speak English. I spent four years at the university in Athens. That's the reason my family agreed to this whole thing. My father was afraid he'd be stuck with an old maid daughter. The only way he could save face was to send me off to America."

Claudio laughed. It was the first time he had ever seen Nicholas at a loss for words. "Then you're in favor of the arrangements, Miss Pappoulis?"

"It's Davonna and, no, I'm not." She turned to Nicholas with a smile. "It's nothing personal, but I think arranged marriages are barbaric! We can write to our families and tell them that we've agreed not to marry, and then we'll be free to go our separate ways. That's acceptable to you, isn't it, Mr. Spiros?"

Nicholas swallowed hard. "Oh, well . . . of course. I've never approved of arranged marriages either."

"Then it's settled." Davonna smiled with relief. "I'm so glad all that awkwardness is over! Now . . . about your import business. Naturally I felt guilty about coming here under false pretenses, so I thought of a way to redeem myself. Before I left Athens, I located a source of fine linen tablecloths, and I also have a list of other items with inexpensive suppliers. If one of you will arrange to deliver my trunk to your office, I'll show you the samples I brought."

Nicholas didn't dare meet his partner's eyes as he picked up Davonna's suitcase and escorted her to his waiting car. Claudio had been right. As Nicholas held open the passenger door and helped Davonna in, he found himself thinking about how wise his father had been.

It had taken seven solid months of candlelight dinners and bouquets of flowers but Nicholas had been nothing if not persistent. There were times when he suspected that he had worn Davonna down by showing her every tourist attraction in town. Now, on December 12, 1941, Davonna, Nicholas, and Claudio sat in the living room of the Spiros flat, celebrating their second anniversary. They were enjoying coffee after dinner and the topic of conversation was the attack on Pearl Harbor five days ago.

"And you think it's foolish to want to defend your adopted country?" Nicholas glared at Claudio. "America's been good to us. It's time we did something in return."

Claudio's face was set as he answered. "I agree it's a noble ambition, but I'm a Sicilian first and an American second."

Davonna filled the men's coffee cups without asking. She knew what was coming.

"I, also, have two countries." Nicholas nodded in agreement. "Don't forget that the Greeks invented democracy. I feel honor-bound to defend it."

"Democracy?" Claudio gave a short laugh. "The Italians invented fascism and imposed peace on the world for a thousand years. No Greek can make a claim like that!" There was a tense silence as the two men glared at each other. Then they smiled sheepishly. They often argued politics but it had never put a strain on their friendship.

Claudio's smile disappeared as he began to see where this conversation was heading. "You didn't do something foolish, did you, Nicholas?"

"Not foolish. Brave." Davonna put her hand on her husband's shoulder. "Nicholas enlisted this morning. He has three days to get his affairs in order before he ships out."

Claudio banged his fist on the table. "That's just what I'd expect from a foolish Greek! It's a good thing I don't have your misguided notions about democracy. Someone has to stay here and mind the business."

"That's what we need to talk about. I want you to buy me out, Claudio. It's not fair to expect you to run the business all by yourself while I share in the profits."

Davonna walked back into the kitchen to make a fresh pot of coffee. It would be a long night. Her husband was a stubborn man. It would take a while to convince Claudio, but eventually he'd see he had no choice but to buy Nicholas out.

While she was waiting for the water to boil, Davonna opened the newspaper and reread the item she'd circled. It was a perfect investment, an old but substantial hotel for sale in New York. Davonna was sure she could talk Nicholas into buying it, and she'd take care of their investment while he was gone. Managing a hotel couldn't be very different from running a large house. For the first time in her life, Davonna was grateful for the compulsory housekeeping training she'd received from her mother.

"Is there more coffee, Davonna?" Nicholas called out from the living room.

"Just a minute, dear. I'm making a fresh pot." Davonna measured out the grounds and set the pot back on the stove. She already had a name for their hotel, the Speer International. It had a nice American ring to it. Of course, Nicholas would laugh when she told him her plans for a world-famous hotel chain, but it would capture his imagination. Davonna was sure that if she and Nicholas worked very hard, the Speer International would become a reality.

1

August 10, 1985

THE SHORT, GRAY-HAIRED man in the expensive sharkskin suit shifted uncomfortably and glanced at his watch. Mike Speer was on the noon flight from Paris and the plane was already twenty minutes late. There wasn't much time to spare.

Calvin Metcalf shivered slightly as he thought of the many times he had waited in this same airport for Mike's father to arrive on the company jet. It seemed impossible that the wasted, desperately ill man Calvin had left this morning had once been such a vital force in the business community. The doctors had refused to commit themselves, but Calvin knew his employer wouldn't last through the day.

The dark-gray limousine with the silver Speer International crest idled in a no-parking zone outside the door, but they still had an hour's drive over gravel roads to the ranch. Nicholas had planned for his death in the same way that he had controlled his empire for the past fifty years, and even the doctors had respected his final wishes. Nicholas had insisted on dying at home. And he had given Calvin strict orders that his son wasn't to be notified until the very last moment.

The other people waiting in the V.I.P. lounge looked

expectant and happy. Calvin drew his linen handkerchief from his pocket. Despite the frigid blast from the air-conditioning, his forehead was damp with sweat.

Only last week two board members at Speer International had instituted a power play and Calvin had learned of their intention to oust the dying president. There was only one way to fight this kind of insubordination and Calvin had already set the wheels in motion. Even though the bylaws of the corporation expressly called for the president's approval, Calvin hadn't discussed his action with Nicholas. Would Mike understand his decision to spare his father? Or was Calvin's career as chief legal counsel to Speer International about to come to an end?

An excited murmur swept through the lounge and several well-dressed people walked over to peer through the huge plate-glass windows. The plane was landing. Calvin took up his position next to the gate and straightened his tie as the first-class passengers began to disembark.

Mike was easy to spot. He towered over the other passengers, tall and handsome in slacks and open-necked silk shirt. As he watched Mike stop to help an attractive woman struggling with two bulging suitcases, Calvin was struck again by the family resemblance between Mike and Nicholas Spiros. Mike was taller by a full six inches but Nicholas claimed he'd been even taller than Mike when he'd set sail from Greece for America in the thirties; something, Nicholas swore it was the salt air, had shrunk him a full foot by the time the ship landed at Ellis Island.

Mike picked up the woman's suitcases effortlessly and placed them in an empty baggage cart. Appearances were deceiving in Mike's case. He moved like a dancer but his slim body hid great strength. The woman was looking up at Mike now, smiling an invitation. He wasn't handsome in the classical sense. His nose was a bit too long for perfection and his eyes were dark and deeply set, crowned with eyebrows just this side of bushy. His dark hair tended to be unruly, even though he kept it cut in a style suggested by Nicholas's own barber, short on top and slightly longer at the sides.

Mike gave the woman a brief smile and moved on. Calvin raised his hand in greeting as Mike's alert brown eyes scanned the crowd. A second later Mike was at his side. "Let's go, Cal!" Mike smiled briefly but his eyes never lost their worried expression.

Cal nodded. "I've arranged for your baggage to be sent on later. Jim's waiting with the car outside."

They hurried toward the exit, Calvin nearly running to keep up with Mike's impatient stride. Mike had grown up in the past year and he had developed his father's commanding presence. As Calvin pushed open the door to the terminal and stepped aside, a single phrase ran through his mind. *The King is dead, long live the King.* It was not the blast of midday Arizona heat that made Calvin blink away tears and draw in his breath sharply.

Mike stood by the pool and gazed up at the huge multicolored sign that obliterated the stars. THE SPEER PALACE. It flashed brilliantly with rows of glittering lights that shifted in intricate patterns. The sign was perfect for the newest, most expensive gambling casino and hotel in Atlantic City, but the heart of the Speer Palace lay in the small bronze plaque that graced the entrance. *In Memory Of Nicholas Spiros 1912–1985.* With the profits he made from the Speer Palace, Mike would open a first-class hotel in every major capital of the world, just as he'd promised his father.

Mike sighed as he gazed around the beautifully landscaped grounds. A year had passed since Nicholas Spiros's death and Mike suspected that, in some ways, he had been a disappointment to his father. He'd done his share of hell-raising during college and he'd never expressed a consuming interest in Speer International. Of course, he'd gone to work as Nicholas's assistant—there had been plenty of opportunity for fun and he'd indulged all his whims in every corner of the world. Now he wished that he'd grown up sooner.

Did every son think of his father as immortal? Mike had never anticipated his father's death. Nicholas Spiros was a survivor. He had prospered during the Depression, survived three years of active service in World War II, and entered the hotel business at just the right time to capitalize on the postwar boom.

Mike stared at the bronze plaque for a moment and thought about the pain his father had endured during his lifetime. Davonna, Mike's mother, had died two weeks after his birth and Nicholas had never remarried. He had tried to keep her memory alive, telling his son stories of how they had met and giving Mike his own album of faded photographs. As a child, Mike hadn't had time to miss his mother. Nicholas had hired the best housekeeper and nanny that money could buy and he was never too busy to take a lonely little boy to the zoo or to spend the afternoon at the park. Mike hadn't realized, until years later, how many business conferences and board meetings had been canceled because of him. Now, as the new president of Speer International, Mike was responsible for the realization of his father's dreams.

Mike was grateful to Cal Metcalf for a number of reasons. He was glad his father had never learned of the board's plot to take over the company from its dying president. With Cal's help, Mike had managed to buy out the two instigators but it had taken a huge chunk of operating capital to do it. Even though Mike knew it was a gamble, he'd put all his eggs in one basket and called it the Speer Palace.

There was work to be done. Mike turned on his heel and walked down the path to the side entrance of the casino. A second later he was inside. He made sure he was smiling as he stopped to watch the action at the blackjack tables. The atmosphere was carefully designed to encourage expensive fun. The last thing Mike wanted his guests to see was a worried face.

It wasn't easy for Mike to smile after the news he'd received this afternoon. They'd paid out another twenty-thousand-dollar jackpot on the quarter slots, the fifteenth this week. Slots were intended to be the casino's bread and butter. They paid the overhead and the odds were usually safe and predictable.

Several women at a nearby table turned to glance at the darkly handsome young man in his well-cut tuxedo. None of them knew they were looking at the owner. Mike had been careful to avoid publicity. It made it easier for him to mingle with his guests and ask them for comments and criticisms.

The crowd from the tour buses completely filled the dollar blackjack section, older women in brightly colored polyester, out for their once-a-year excursion to the excitement and bright lights of Atlantic City. As

Mike stepped closer, Bobby Marrin, the newest dealer on the shift, explained the rules to one of the ladies at his table. "It's a little complicated at first, but I'll be happy to help you. I'm required to draw another card if my total is sixteen or less. And I have to stand on seventeen or over. Do you know how to count up your hand?"

The woman shook her head and looked embarrassed. "We've never played before. Are you sure you have the time to teach us?"

"I've got all the time in the world, ma'am. We want you to have fun. Just remember that face cards and tens count ten. Aces can be either one or eleven. That's up to you. And the other cards are just what they say. You try to get as close to twenty-one as you can, without going over."

All six women nodded gravely. The woman in the flowered pantsuit seemed to be the leader of the group. "Then you have eighteen?"

"Right!" Bobby nodded. "A queen and an eight. You're catching on really fast, ma'am. Now add up your cards."

"Four and six. I have ten. Does that mean I should take another card?"

"Right again!" Bobby flashed his grin. "Another card can do nothing but improve your hand."

Bobby dealt her another card, an ace.

"That's eleven . . . or . . . twenty-one! Do I win?"

"You certainly do!"

The woman's friends squealed in excitement and she smiled up at Bobby as he counted out her winnings. Bobby grinned back. He seemed genuinely happy for her, just as happy as if she'd toked him the way most experienced blackjack players would. Mike made a mental note to move Bobby to the higher limit tables, where the tokes were better. He had a good rapport with the guests.

Mike pulled up the cuff of his jacket and glanced at his watch. It was nine in the evening and the high rollers would drift in soon, taxiing from casino to casino searching for the best odds in town while their wives enjoyed the shows.

There were no clocks in the public section of the Speer Palace, a deliberate omission. It was part of the creation of a timeless ambience where guests could play for hours without realizing that dawn was approaching and ordinary people were home in bed. Night or day, the interior of the casino looked the same. Gold satin drapes were hung in strategic spots, giving the illusion of windows. Of course, there were banks of windows near the slots, but that was to attract the foot traffic from the street.

Mike's first experience with American casinos had been unpleasant. He'd felt assaulted by the glitter, the noise and the flashing lights. He had enjoyed the gaming salons in Europe, where the atmosphere was hushed and refined. The Speer Palace was a combination of the two cultures. The outer section was filled with what Mike called cheap thrills. There were slot machines with ringing bells, a giant keno board that flashed in a strobe effect when the numbers were drawn, and a noisy bar where drinks were a dollar and gorgeous waitresses in skimpy costumes delivered gigantic shrimp cocktails to the tables. The drinks and the shrimp were loss leaders. The Speer Palace took a bath on both items, but the lure of inexpensive booze and cheap food brought people into the casino. And once they were inside, they couldn't resist trying their luck.

"Paging Mr. Browne. Mr. Sam Browne. Please meet your party in the Royal Bar." "Sam Browne" was the code name for the security force at the casino. Casino codes were designed to sound like ordinary telephone pages. Mike watched as two security guards, dressed in conventional suits and ties, arrived at the bar. After a hurried conversation with the bartender, they smilingly escorted a man in a plaid shirt to the main door. There was no fuss and no commotion. No one, not even the girl sitting on an adjacent bar stool, noticed that the man had been evicted.

"Anything I can do?" Flip Warner came around the corner of a bank of dollar slots and hurried to Mike's side. "I heard the page."

"Everything's taken care of, Flip." Mike smiled at his friend and employee. At thirty-two, Flip had a boyish look that caused him to be carded in most of the other casinos in Atlantic City. He was barely five-feet-seven, and he usually wore boots to add another couple of inches to his height. His baby-blue eyes and innocent expression had marked him for an easy target when he and Mike had been roommates at Thorton Military Academy until he'd learned to fend for himself quite capably.

"How's the 'Eye in the Sky,' Flip?" Mike was careful not to look up and draw attention to the dark strip of ceiling above the gambling pits. It concealed a room equipped with video cameras and a team of spotters, hired to watch for any irregularity at the tables. The Speer Palace spotters were employees who watched the action at the pits, alert for cheaters on both sides of the table. Even though the casino dealers knew they were being watched, occasionally someone tried to outsmart the surveillance.

"Everything's normal tonight. We've got a couple of counters at table fourteen, but so far they've had lousy luck."

"There's nothing illegal about counting cards. Just keep an eye on them to make sure they don't slow down the game."

Flip nodded. "Dale Fratkin told me a good one tonight. He swears that Connie's Casino on the Boardwalk has nozzles over the poker tables. The old man pulls a switch about two in the morning and gives everyone a couple of minutes of pure oxygen. Dale says the players wake right up and go on gambling all night."

Mike began to smile. He'd heard that story about every big casino in Nevada. "Tell Dale we don't need to do anything like that in the Speer Palace. If our poker players start yawning, we send Natasha over to take their drink orders. She's enough to wake the dead."

"I'll tell him." Flip laughed. "I'm going to stop by the blackjack tables first to check out the new shill we hired. Then I'll be back upstairs if you need me."

Mike watched Flip walk away, hoping the new girl would work out better than the last. A pretty girl was hired to sit at an empty blackjack table to start the action. All the shill had to do was have a good time playing with the casino's money and draw other gamblers to the tables. There was only one occupational hazard: occasionally a girl got greedy, especially if she'd won a lot of money that she had to give right back to the casino.

Flip had been suspicious of the last girl and he'd watched until he'd caught her cheating with a dealer. The scam involved a hollow case that looked, from the room above the pits, like three hundred-dollar chips. The girl bet heavily until she lost a hand for three hundred-dollar chips. The dealer picked up the phony stack, slipped it over three two-dollar chips that he'd gotten as tokes, and replaced it in the rack. His count was correct when the chips were tallied, and he was safe as long as no one tried to separate the hundreds. After the tally, the dealer slipped off the case and passed it back to the girl who had already pocketed the real hundred-dollar chips. Flip had studied the video tape until he'd spotted the scam, and without his help, the drain on the Speer Palace could have gone on indefinitely.

The baccarat tables were in a secluded alcove near the lounge. Mike strolled past and nodded to Sir Alfred, his most distinguished dealer. Sir Alfred was just plain Alf Connors when he came to work for Mike four months ago, but his English accent had given Mike an inspiration. A bit of gray at his temples, applied by the cosmetologist in the beauty shop downstairs, and an expensively tailored suit with a monogrammed silk handkerchief in the breast pocket provided just the touch of class the casino needed. Most of the guests at the Speer Palace felt honored when Sir Alfred took their money.

There was an excited murmur from one of the crap tables and Mike walked over. A man in a ten-gallon hat was controlling the dice. From the reaction of the crowd it was plain to see that he was on a roll. The head croupier smiled as the man rolled again and raked in a big pile of chips. Mike nodded. He had instructed his personnel to compliment the players when they were winning and commiserate with them when they lost.

The odds were always in the casino's favor and they would more than recoup any losses by the end of the night.

"Could I get something for you, Mr. Speer?" A cocktail waitress in a red satin costume brushed up close to him and flashed her sexiest smile. Mike grinned as he remembered what Amy had told him. A group of his cocktail waitresses had an ongoing contest. They each contributed a dollar a night to a kitty. The one who managed to get the first date with him won the money.

"Ginger ale in a tall glass. There's no hurry. You'll find me by the poker tables."

The Speer Palace was hosting several conventions this week. Two delegates were standing by an empty table, talking to the pit boss. The man wearing the HI, I'M LARRY! nametag was protesting the house limits at the poker tables.

"I'll take care of it, Henry." Mike nodded to the pit boss. "Were you looking for a high-stake game, Larry?"

"I sure was," Larry grumbled. "We play for more money than this back home in Milwaukee."

"The Speer Palace runs a private game with a five-hundred-dollar buy-in for our special guests. Does that sound about right?"

Larry grinned and patted his pocket. "That's perfect. I got a bankroll from some of the guys back home."

"Just go past the bank of dollar slots and turn right when you come to the roulette wheels. There's an alcove off to your right with a mahogany door. Tell the man outside that Mike Speer sent you and he'll be glad to find you a spot."

Larry looked impressed as he realized he was talking

to the owner. "Gee thanks, Mr. Speer. I really appreciate this."

"Here's your drink, Mr. Speer." The cocktail waitress came back with Mike's ginger ale. "I'm through with my shift in an hour. Is there anything else you need tonight?"

"No, thanks. That's all." Mike gave her a smile. She looked disappointed, and Mike wondered just how big that kitty had gotten over the past few weeks. As he lifted the glass, Mike noticed a message written on the back of his cocktail napkin: Mike—please call me. Lottie: 555-3073. He laughed. Lottie was definitely out to win.

It was time to put a stop to the contest. Mike slipped through a door behind one of the gold curtains and walked down the carpeted hallway to the office suites. The door to Amy Warner's office was open and she was sitting behind her desk, phone to her ear, staring out at the pool below.

Mike grinned as he stood in the doorway, watching. She was facing the other direction and she hadn't heard his approach, obviously concentrating on her phone call. "That's crazy, Roy! We can get another top act for that money and they'll be every bit as good as the Dynamos. There's no way we're going to throw in five suites!"

Amy shook her head and her gorgeous blond hair swung like a shining wave. Sometimes Mike had trouble resisting the urge to reach out and touch it. Amy was a beautiful woman all the way around, tall and rounded in all the right places, with soft smooth skin like ivory satin.

Mike brought himself up short. He was lucky to have Amy for a friend and she was perfect as the Speer

Palace personnel director. Of course, he'd noticed that Amy had a crush on him when she was growing up and he'd been very careful not to give her the wrong idea. He wasn't the type of a guy to take advantage of his best friend's baby sister, especially after Flip had told him Amy'd been living with a man in New York. According to Flip, wedding bells were about to ring when the whole romance had turned sour. Amy hadn't wanted to discuss the details and Flip hadn't pressed the issue, but the man was now married to someone else. Flip said that was why Amy had jumped at the chance to work for Mike at the Speer Palace and get out of New York as fast as she could.

Flip had asked Mike to keep an eye on Amy to make sure she didn't fall in love with some wolf on the rebound and Mike had done just that, wisely keeping his distance when she'd dropped a few hints about dating *him.* He took her out for dinner occasionally and tried to be a good friend. Only in private did he admit to himself that it would be much easier to maintain a platonic friendship if Amy weren't so damned attractive.

Amy laughed, a low soft sound, swiveled around in her chair, and shot Mike a smile. "New Year's Eve? I'll have to check the bookings and get back to you on that, Roy. Now tell me exactly what you need and I'll check into it. And forget the extra perks. Nobody but Duran Duran would rate five extra suites!"

Mike took a deep breath. New Year's Eve. It was funny how it all came back to him. Amy had just turned seventeen and he was visiting the Warners for the holidays. They had planned to go out for dinner and dancing to celebrate that night but his date had canceled at the last minute. Amy's cousin hadn't been able to make it either and he found himself escorting Amy.

She had been gorgeous. Mike still remembered the low-cut dress she'd worn.

"Hello, Mike." Amy scribbled a note on her pad and looked up at him with her incredibly blue eyes. "What can I do for you?"

"Oh! Uh . . . there was something I wanted to ask you."

Mike blinked hard and forced the memories of that summer out of his mind. It was a damn good thing he'd been older and wiser than Amy. "It's that idiotic cocktail waitress contest, Amy. I think the whole thing's getting out of hand. A girl named Lottie slipped me her phone number tonight."

"Are you upset because she doesn't want you for yourself?" Amy smiled sweetly.

"Okay, okay." Mike grinned. "Maybe my ego is getting in the way just a little, but we've got to do something about it, Amy. They're supposed to be paying attention to the guests, not to me!"

"You could ask one of them for a date and split the money with her."

Amy held up her hand as she saw the expression on Mike's face. "Just kidding, Boss. I know how you feel about dating the employees. I'll figure something out. Just leave it to me."

"You're a peach, Amy." Mike grinned. "I couldn't run this place without you and Flip. If you haven't eaten yet, I'll buy you a hamburger to show my appreciation."

Amy laughed. Mike was a real hamburger fanatic. Chef Sussman in the Dome Room turned positively green when Mike ordered one of his specialties. Mike's latest invention was a hamburger on whole-wheat bread with peanut butter and plum jam. Before that it had been sour cream and black olives.

"Can I take a rain check for tomorrow night? Tony's running tryouts for the new floor show and I promised him I'd be there."

"Sure." Mike headed for the door. "Seven o'clock tomorrow. I'll tell Chef Sussman to pull out all the stops. Maybe he'll whip up a burger with cream cheese and anchovies."

Amy made a face and Mike laughed. He wasn't sure why he felt so disappointed as he left her office. He certainly hadn't planned a romantic evening. They were friends, good friends, that was all.

Mike was alert as he went back on the floor and walked past the row of electronic slots. Everything looked perfectly normal but Mike suspected that someone was rigging the slots to beat the system even though it was quite a trick. They were programmed for a strict payoff percentage and there were no moving parts inside the case. The traditional slots had from three to five wheels that started to spin when the player pulled down the handle. It was a mechanical system and the jackpots were controlled by the number of bars and lucky sevens on each wheel. The casino maintenance crew checked the wheels and replaced them when they started to wear but the electronic machines were solid state. The manufacturer claimed they were tamperproof.

Percentages were the most critical aspect of the casino business. Each game had its own, and Mike checked the numbers every night. If the house take on blackjack was low for one week, it would even out the next. Of course there were occasional big winners, the reason the casinos stayed in business. But the losers who followed a big winner brought the casino percentage right back to a normal level again. Mike knew the percentages never lied. If the Speer Palace's electronic slots were paying off at a rate above their programmed percentage, there was only one conclusion. Someone was cheating.

In his blackest moments, Mike was convinced that the Speer Palace was jinxed. His troubles had started almost immediately. There was a long strike during construction and a massive runaround in getting the necessary permits from the city. Deliveries of furnishings had been late and the Speer Palace had opened its doors six months after the projected date. During the past four months, all sorts of things had gone wrong. A shipment of chips had been hijacked and Mike had been forced to change his imprint and order new supplies. And only last week he'd discovered two of his bartenders with their hands in the till. Almost every day new problems arose and it took time and money to solve them. Mike tried to convince himself that it was just a run of bad luck but it seemed to be getting worse with each passing day.

"A telephone call for Mrs. Jeffries. Mrs. Valerie Jeffries. A telephone call."

Mike grinned as he recognized Alice Plotnik's voice. Alice was the best of his "heavenly voices." She was in her fifties, a short gray-haired woman who weighed in at over two hundred pounds, but she sounded incredibly sexy. She was the night supervisor in the communications room, the small three-person cubicle on the second floor of the casino that housed the switchboard. Yesterday, a regular at the casino had confessed that he always had a friend page him at the Speer Palace just so Alice would call out his name.

"A telephone call for Mrs. Jeffries. Mrs. Valerie Jeffries, a telephone call."

Mrs. Jeffries wasn't answering her page. Mike knew that Alice would write the message on a card and send it to the front desk with the runner who made hourly pickups at the communications room. If he saw Mrs. Jeffries, he'd tell her that she had a message. The middle-aged widow deserved V.I.P. treatment—she'd been married to one of the most influential oil men in Texas.

"Paging Mr. Pike. Mr. Lance Pike."

Mike headed toward the bank of white house phones. That was his page and it usually meant trouble somewhere in the casino. Mike was never paged by his real name. Too many people wanted to contact the owner of the Speer Palace for various reasons. He didn't want to be surrounded by curious guests when he answered the phone.

"Alice? Mike Speer."

"Stan called in for you. He says Rick Dwyer is trying to pick up Mrs. Jeffries in the Dome. He thought you'd like to take care of it personally."

"Thanks, Alice. I'm on my way."

The view was spectacular as the glass elevator rose to the twenty-first floor above the neon lights of the city. There was a view from every table, and most of the sightseers stayed for dinner and drinks. When they paid their bill, they were given a chip that was good for one two-dollar bet at the blackjack tables downstairs. Few people could resist something that was free and nobody could walk away from the tables after only one hand.

Mike spotted Valerie Jeffries at the bar. Rick Dwyer was sitting next to her, arm draped possessively around her shoulders.

Mike approached them with a smile on his face. "Hello, Mrs. Jeffries. I just heard a telephone page for you and I thought it might be important." He gestured toward the bank of house phones against the far wall. "If you pick up one of the white phones in the alcove, Alice will read you the message."

"Thank you, Mr. Speer." Valerie Jeffries gave him a warm smile and slid off her bar stool. "I'm flattered. What did I do to rate your personal attention?"

"Perhaps it's your dress. It's almost as lovely as you are."

"Oh, Mr. Speer!" Valerie laughed and floated off in a cloud of ice-blue chiffon, a diamond clip nestled in her elaborate hairdo. Valerie Jeffries was an important guest and Mike wanted to make sure she had an enjoyable stay at the Speer Palace. It was just unfortunate that she had chosen Rick Dwyer for her companion.

Mike waited until Valerie was well away from the bar. "Having fun, Rick?"

Rick Dwyer shifted uncomfortably on the bar stool. "Uh . . . sure, Mr. Speer."

"That's good. It was nice of you to entertain Mrs. Jeffries but she's a personal friend of mine."

Rick reached for his handkerchief and wiped his forehead, looking very nervous now. "I'm sorry, Mr. Speer. I didn't know. Uh . . . will you tell her that I had to leave unexpectedly?"

"Sure thing, Rick. Why don't you try the Marina? I hear there's a whole busload of rich widows from New York. You ought to be able to find one who'll pay your price."

Mike kept an eye on Rick until the elevator doors had closed behind him. Then he crossed to his reserved table at the back of the room and picked up the private phone on the banquette. "Alice? It's Mike Speer. Tell security to page me if they see Rick Dwyer in here again tonight." He hung up the phone and turned to the waitress who was hovering by his table, just out of earshot. She was good, polite and attentive without being intrusive. He'd have to remember to compliment her supervisor. "Will you bring a bottle of Dom Pérignon with two glasses? And ask Mrs. Jeffries if she'd care to join me."

In less than a minute the waitress was back with the champagne. "Shall I open it now, Mr. Speer? Mrs. Jeffries said she'd be delighted." Mike grinned and made a mental note of her name. Trish. She opened the bottle with a minimum of effort, gently dislodging the cork. The loud pop and the foamy fizz were all Hollywood theatricals. Trish knew the proper way to open an expensive bottle of champagne.

Valerie appeared just as the waitress was filling her glass. Mike stood to greet her. "I'm sorry, but Mr. Dwyer was called away. Would you care to join me for a glass of champagne?"

Valerie Jeffries smiled, a brilliant flash of white in her deeply tanned face. She was the soul of composure as she settled her skirt around her and accepted the glass Mike held out to her. "Mr. Dwyer was called away suddenly?"

Mike nodded.

"With a little nudge by the owner of the Speer Palace, perhaps?"

Mike nodded again.

"Oh, well!" Valerie sighed and took a sip of her champagne. "I suspected all along that he was a gigolo but hope beats eternal, Mr. Speer. I haven't been approached by such an attractive young man in longer than I care to admit."

Mike couldn't help it. He started to grin. Surely Valerie Jeffries must realize that she was still a very desirable woman!

"I can't believe that, Mrs. Jeffries. You could have any man in this room."

"Including the one at this table?"

Mike threw back his head and laughed. He needn't have worried about Rick Dwyer. He raised his glass in a salute. "Absolutely!"

Valerie touched the rim of her glass against his and gazed straight into his eyes. "Well, then, Mr. Speer. Let's toast my protected virtue. And anything else you might have in mind."

Mike grinned as she reached for him again. Flip had been right. He'd needed a little relaxation. He hadn't felt this good in a long time.

Valerie Jeffries was simply amazing—sexy, spontaneous, and completely tireless. And if he wasn't careful, she'd wear him out. She moaned as his hand moved down to brush over the silky curls of hair and her legs spread open eagerly, thighs trembling with anticipation. Mike ran his fingers through the slick wetness that coated the pink valley between her legs and she drew in her breath sharply, thrusting herself up against his hand. "Oh, Mike!" she gasped. "Don't quit on me now!"

Mike withdrew his hand. Her hair had come loose from the diamond clip that had held it in place and it spread across the pillow in a shining dark cloud.

"Again?" Mike smiled down at her.

"Yes . . . please!" Her voice was low and throaty, ending in a gasp as he entered her just far enough to tease. She threw her legs around his back, attempting to pull him in deeper.

Mike held himself aloof, just penetrating her steamy warmth as she squirmed beneath him. He could feel her heat growing and it was all he could do to hold out just a little longer. Valerie whimpered, hips lifting high from the mattress as she struggled to capture him.

"Mike! Please?"

Her body turned soft and sweet beneath his. The compulsion to possess her was unbearable. Mike gasped and drove forward with a powerful thrust. Valerie shuddered once and her center turned to molten lava clinging and surrounding his hardness. She cried out sharply and trembled as passion erased the last vestiges of her composure. There was a long moment of silence and then Valerie laughed. Mike looked down at her with a question in his eyes.

"Benjamin Franklin wrote a letter of advice to a young man. He advised him to choose an older woman for his mistress because older women were so grateful."

Mike chuckled. "I could counter with the line about women and fine wines. It's true. You were wonderful."

Valerie smiled and snuggled closer to him. Then she gave a gasp of amazement. "I don't believe it! Again?"

Her mascara had smudged and her hair was a mass of

tangles. She looked far more desirable than she had in the lounge with hairdo and makeup intact.

"We've got all night, Mrs. Jeffries." Mike began to move, long slow strokes that brought the wildness back to her eyes.

"It's Val," she breathed as she lifted her legs and locked them around his back.

2

MIKE STUCK HIS head out the door of 2015 and peered down the hallway. No one was in sight. He stepped out quickly and closed the door soundlessly behind him. He'd stop at the florists and order a yellow rose for Valerie's breakfast tray. Charged with energy, Mike realized he was whistling as he walked toward the elevator. He stopped abruptly. It was almost four in the morning and some of his guests would be sleeping.

There was a room-service tray outside room 2017. Mike glanced at the tray as he walked past. It contained the remnants of a steak dinner and a half-finished glass of red wine. It was possible to order full meals from room service twenty-four hours a day. Mike knew the tray had been placed there after three A.M. His staff had orders to pick up the trays every hour to keep the corridor tidy.

Another tray with an ice bucket and an empty bottle of champagne was outside room 2021. Three glasses, two with lipstick on the rims. A *ménage à trois?* It certainly couldn't have been more exciting than his evening with Mrs. Jeffries.

A pair of gleaming shoes were placed neatly outside the door to 2025. There was no extra charge for the service. Mike paid Jake Patterson, his shoeshine man, an hourly rate and most guests left a tip as well. Jake was happier at the Speer Palace than he'd been at his stand in the bus depot. He said the shoes at the Palace had more class.

The Speer Palace tried to provide every service a guest might want, from a one-hour dry cleaners to a beauty parlor and barber shop. There was a seamstress on duty to help guests with last-minute alterations on clothes from the boutique downstairs, and a floral shop that delivered direct or wired flowers to any state in the union: a miniature city on the lower level of the hotel, open twenty-four hours a day.

Mike took the elevator down to the lower level and ordered Valerie's rose. Then he used the escalator to get to the lobby and switched to the private elevator that took him up to the twenty-second floor. Mike's quarters were in sharp contrast to the glamorously appointed suites on the lower floors. There were four bedrooms, a conventional kitchen, a rustic living room, and a patio roof garden that resembled the backyard of a suburban rambler. His father had escaped from the world of big business by building his ranch house in Arizona. Mike had accomplished a similar feat at the top of the Speer Palace. He knew he had to stay at the Palace to run his business but his home on the twenty-second floor was his retreat.

Mike turned on the lights in the hallway and picked up his stack of personal mail. There was a brown envelope from Cal Metcalf, containing Speer International's quarterly profit-and-loss statement. No surprises there; Speer International had shown a healthy profit. The only branch losing money was the Speer Palace. Mike knew that if he didn't show a profit by the end of the next quarter he'd have to go to the board for additional reserves, but when they'd approved his plans for the casino, Mike had agreed to their time limit. He had two months to show a profit or the casino and hotel would be sold.

The rest of Mike's mail consisted of invitations to send for a "genuine diamondlike" ring for the incredible price of nine ninety-five, join the videotape-of-the-month club, contribute to the foundation for psychic research, and buy personalized Christmas cards now, at the off-season rates. One official-looking letter informed him that he'd won a prize in a sweepstakes, which could be claimed by driving to Perfect Pines, a dude ranch fifty miles from Atlantic City, to attend a short sales presentation. His prize would be one of the items listed in column A: one million dollars, a new Mercedes convertible, or a transistor radio.

One by one, Mike dropped the envelopes into the hall wastebasket, almost missing the postcard at the bottom of the stack. The picture showed an expensive-looking apartment building in Manhattan, complete with a doorman in red livery trimmed with gold braid. Mike turned it over and laughed out loud as he read the message.

Still at the same old address but today I met a woman who lives here. Give me a week. There was no signature but Mike recognized Jack Humphries's handwriting. Mike, Flip, and Jack had been best buddies at Thorton Academy. Mike propped up the card on the hall table to show to Flip and Amy tomorrow, then went to change clothes.

Mike's bedroom was immense, with two mirrored walk-in closets and sliding glass doors that opened onto the patio. Mike's tribute to "The Duke" covered one wall. There were movie posters of John Wayne and

Henry Fonda in *Fort Apache,* John Wayne and James Stewart in *The Man Who Shot Liberty Valance,* John Wayne and Natalie Wood in *The Searchers,* John Wayne and Victor McLaglen in *She Wore a Yellow Ribbon,* and John Wayne and Maureen O'Hara in *Rio Grande* and *The Quiet Man.* The adjoining wall was devoted to other John Ford films. There were twenty-six full-sized posters in all, but the room was so large there was still plenty of space for Mike's soccer trophies and the beer steins he'd brought back from Europe. He had a mini-gym in one corner and Mike sighed as he looked at the expensive equipment he rarely used. His hours at the casino were long, and when he got back to his quarters the last thing he felt like doing was lifting weights.

Ten minutes later Mike had showered and dressed in an old warm-up suit. He tossed his tuxedo into a bag for the cleaners and padded, barefoot, into the living room. He knew he should be exhausted but the hours he'd spent with Valerie had left him too keyed up to go straight to bed.

The living room was paneled in knotty pine, the ceiling rising to a peak with exposed rafters. One wall was made entirely of glass, giving him a view of the Boardwalk at night that he loved.

Despite the glass wall, the room had a homey feel. It was filled with overstuffed furniture and there was an old kerosene lamp hanging from a hook over the comfortable brown and orange plaid couch. The lantern was at least a hundred years old and it had hung in the original bunkhouse of his father's ranch in Arizona. Mike had planned this room carefully and it was a study in contrasts. An antique gramophone cabinet with a crank on the side contained his modern stereo system and an antique wooden icebox effectively camouflaged a small, modern refrigerator that serviced the old-fashioned saloon bar.

At the touch of a button the huge floor-to-ceiling painting of Dodge City at the turn of the century slid back to reveal his giant-screen television and video recorder. Watching a John Ford film always relaxed him.

No movie was complete without a snack and Mike walked down the hallway to the kitchen pantry and surveyed the shelves filled with junk food. There were packages of Twinkies, Scooter Pies, Doritos, onion-flavored potato chips, red licorice whips, beer nuts, everything one might find at a theater concession stand. Perhaps it was the effect of being raised on fine gourmet cuisine, but Mike was addicted to junk food. After a moment of contemplation he settled on a bag of cheese popcorn and a box of Junior Mints, the perfect complement to his movie. Then he went back to the living room and examined his collection of John Ford films. He had watched *The Quiet Man* last night and *The Searchers* the night before. Mike slipped his favorite cassette, *She Wore a Yellow Ribbon,* in the video tape machine. Watching John Wayne kill Indians ought to cheer him up.

Mike settled down in his favorite chair, munching popcorn. John Ford certainly knew how to get a performance out of an actor. Rumor had it that the Duke and Ford had yelled at each other before every scene in this movie, but whether or not that was true was beside the point. Mike thought John Wayne's portrayal of Captain Brittles was one of his best roles.

Even though the movie was every bit as wonderful as he had remembered, Mike found his mind wandering.

The slot machine cheater. The hijacking of his chips. The trouble with the city permits. The whole thing was like a giant jigsaw puzzle. If he could only put the pieces together in the right order, he might be able to figure out who was trying to sabotage the Speer Palace.

Even Victor McLaglen, taking on half the regiment in an archetypical bar room fight, failed to shake his depression. Mike switched off the video recorder and sighed deeply. He needed a friend, not an exciting companion like Valerie Jeffries, but a real friend, someone he could burden with his problems. The moment he thought of it, Mike was slipping on his shoes. Amy stayed up late most nights. He could drive past her apartment and stop in for a visit. Perhaps he could even persuade her to join him for the rest of the movie.

The streets of Atlantic City were filled with traffic, even at four in the morning. Mike rolled down the windows on his Porsche and let the wind whip past his face. He felt better already, just doing something.

Amy lived in a two-bedroom apartment in a residential section of the city, two miles away from the bright lights and glitter of the casinos. Most casino employees lived in the residential section of the city, as far away from the Boardwalk or the Marina as they could get. Mike understood. Eight hours of coping with people who were in a party mood and being inundated by ringing bells and flashing lights were enough for anyone. It was a schizophrenic life, alternating between the noise and the bright lights of a continuous celebration and the suburban home with crabgrass and plumbing problems, but Mike was grateful there were enough people who seemed to enjoy this divided life to fill the jobs at the Speer Palace.

Mike drove past Amy's apartment slowly. Her car was in her parking space and a light was on in her living room. He parked the Porsche at the curb and walked up the sidewalk to her door. He had just raised his hand to knock when he thought better of it. What would he say when she answered the door? She'd be sure to ask why he was awake so late and he'd never lied to her. Mike felt vaguely guilty, realizing he didn't want to tell Amy about his night with Valerie Jeffries.

Twenty minutes later, when Mike was home in bed, it occurred to him to wonder what Amy was doing awake at four in the morning. Did she have a boyfriend he didn't know about? The thought of Amy in some stranger's arms wasn't pleasant at all.

Amy glanced at the clock as the Porsche drove away. She had almost opened the door and invited him in but her pride had stopped her. There were no secrets among the staff in the Speer Palace.

The letter she'd stayed up so late to write lay unsealed on the coffee table. Amy took it out of the envelope and read the beginning again. *Steve—I don't love you and I couldn't marry you even if you were free. I'm sorry you believe your marriage was a mistake but if you insist on coming to Atlantic City, I can't see you.*

Her words sounded cruel and there was no hint of the closeness she'd shared with Steve. She'd written at least a dozen drafts of the note but this was the best she could do. After all, they'd settled it all seven months ago when she'd moved out of the brownstone they'd shared in New York.

Steve's letter had been waiting for her when she'd come home from work. After the past months of living alone, Amy missed him dreadfully, especially tonight when her own desires seemed so hopeless. They'd laughed a lot in the year they'd spent together and the sex had been good. It had all blown up last January when Steve had asked her to marry him and Amy had finally realized that she'd been fooling not only Steve but herself. She could never marry him.

Amy picked up the crumpled balls of notepaper and tossed them into the wastebasket. She'd been tempted to encourage Steve and she knew how unfair that would be. She had deluded herself long enough. She was in love with Mike Speer and she was determined to make him love her back.

She really had to get some sleep. Amy climbed into bed and turned off the light. It was four-thirty in the morning and she had to get up again at eleven to make her meeting with Mike at noon. As personnel director of the Speer Palace, Amy frequently worked a twelve-hour day, six days a week. Even though Sundays were theoretically her day off, there was always a crisis or two to handle. It usually added up to more than a seventy-hour week.

There was a thump as Amy's cat raced across the room and landed on the foot of the bed. The little calico was good company. She always gave a little meow of welcome when Amy unlocked the door and it was comforting to reach out at night to cuddle a purring cat. "Come on, Katy." Amy picked her up and snuggled her a little. "You can stay if you're ready to sleep but I'm too tired to play."

Katy stared at her for a moment, head cocked to the side. Then she swished her tail and jumped off the bed to pad back to the living room. Amy was very glad she'd rescued Katy when she spotted the half-starved little calico trying to raid a garbage can behind the

Speer Palace. Since there were strict rules about keeping pets in her apartment building, Amy had put Katy in a cardboard box and smuggled her in at three A.M. So far none of her neighbors suspected that she had an illegal pet.

Amy tried to sleep, but scenes from the past came back to haunt her. She had a vivid memory of her mother, coming in to tuck her under the covers before going out to a dinner party. Even now she could visualize her mother's face, her eyes matching the deep sea-green of her gown and crinkling at the corners when she smiled. Amy remembered reaching up to hug her, asking for one last bedtime story. Her mother had read *Goldilocks,* doing all the voices exactly the way Amy had loved; Baby Bear was a high-pitched squeak that always made Amy giggle. Amy had recited Goldilocks's lines from memory and her mother had told her she looked just like the pretty blond girl in the story. Years later, her father had told her they'd been late for the party because her mother had insisted on reading that one last story.

Amy had another vivid memory, one that she did her best to push to the back of her mind. Three years old, she'd just come in from playing in the snow and Clara, the housekeeper, had given her a cup of hot cocoa. Clara had answered the phone and, when Amy'd asked her why she was crying, Clara had picked her up and called her "poor little darling."

The funeral was a blur of images, cold wet snowflakes blowing against her face, tall granite gravestones surrounded by leafless trees and a man in a black coat reading big words that Amy didn't understand. Her father had cried and she had stood next to him, holding his hand and Flip's tightly. She'd been too young to realize what had happened but she'd cried, too. Even now, tears occasionally came to Amy's eyes when she caught the scent of a woman wearing *Joy*, her mother's favorite perfume. Amy rolled over, switched on the light, and got out of bed. There was only one cure for the late-night blues and it was lucky she'd stopped at the grocery store on the way home tonight. There was a whole carton of double chocolate fudge fantasy ice cream in the freezer.

In less than a minute Amy was back under the covers, ice cream carton in one hand, spoon in the other, and a meowing cat at the foot of the bed. She put the lid of the carton down on the floor for Katy to lick, and smiled. Her spirits were beginning to perk up already.

Amy had always gone after what she'd wanted. It had started when she'd asked her father for a ten-speed just like Flip's for her sixth birthday. Of course her father had explained that it was impossible for such a little girl to ride a ten-speed like her older brother's. Why, she couldn't even reach the pedals. He could buy her a nice little girl's bike, with training wheels if that was what she wanted. Amy had been insistent. She'd wanted a ten-speed and nothing else would do. If she could learn to ride Flip's, would her father change his mind? There was no use arguing with Amy once her mind was made up. Her father had reluctantly agreed. He hadn't counted on Amy's determined streak. The next day Amy had pestered Flip until he'd given in. He'd promised to help but she mustn't be disappointed if she couldn't do it. Together, they'd rigged up extensions for Amy's shoes so she could reach the pedals.

The first day of practice had been a disaster. Amy'd skinned both knees but she'd been up, bright and early the next day, to try it again. By the time her birthday rolled around she was peppered with Band-Aids but she'd gotten her very own ten-speed.

When Amy was twelve, her determination had come out in full force again. She had wanted to go away to boarding school with her friends but Flip was attending college and she couldn't bear to leave her father all alone in their big house with only the housekeeper for company. The perfect solution was to find a nice woman for her father to marry but Amy knew he was still grieving for her mother.

Amy had written to "Dear Abby," explaining the problem, and her letter had been published in the daily newspaper. Luckily, she'd spotted it first and torn out the page before her father'd had a chance to see it. Amy had reread the column several times and everything Abby had said made sense. Abby had said that extended grief was not a healthy emotion. Amy had known it was up to her to help her father learn to enjoy his life again.

Amy had noticed that her father seemed to be most cheerful when he worked on a project with Rita Williams, his administrative assistant. Rita was always friendly when Amy visited the office and she had a special drawer in her desk. Inside was a notepad that said, FROM THE DESK OF AMY WARNER, an assortment of colored felt-tip pens, and a whole collection of rubber stamps with an ink pad. Rita smiled a lot and she had glossy curly black hair. Amy thought Rita was pretty for an older woman. She had asked, before she'd learned it was a social *faux pas,* and Rita had said she was thirty-two. Her father was ten years older and that made them perfect for each other.

Right before Amy's twelfth Christmas, she had started her campaign in earnest. She'd asked her father if he could give Rita the afternoon off to help Amy shop for Christmas. Rita had such good taste and Amy wanted her presents to be perfect this year. Perhaps her father could meet them downtown around seven?

Of course Amy had asked that Rita be included in their Christmas plans—after all, she had helped to pick out the presents. And New Year's Eve wouldn't be fun at all if Rita didn't come with them to Times Square.

Amy had spent the next two months arranging outings to the zoo, the movies, ice skating, the park, a musical, the science museum, the modern art museum, and the natural history museum. Naturally, everything was much more fun if Rita came along. When Amy had gone as far as she could along those lines, she'd started in on the home front.

Wouldn't it be good for her father's business if he had occasional dinner parties at home? Amy had volunteered to be his hostess, sure Rita would be willing to teach her the things young ladies needed to know. Dinner parties were duly given and return invitations had come in the mail. Rita and her father had become a couple in the eyes of society and before the year was out, Amy's father had asked what she'd thought about Rita joining their family.

Amy pointed out there was only one problem. She'd read in *Redbook* that newlyweds should have time alone, adjustments and all that. Would her father please send her to boarding school for a year? She'd really love to go.

Boarding school was wonderful and Amy had loved it. She hadn't had to use her determined streak again until the end of her junior year when it was time to pick the foreign language she wanted to take. Amy had vacillated between French and Italian and made up her mind to take both. She'd promised to work hard and there was room in her schedule. The guidance counselor had told Amy it was impossible. Amy had stubbornly insisted. If she got her father to sign the consent form, they'd let her take both, wouldn't they?

Her father had laughed when he'd signed the form. He was well acquainted with Amy's determined streak. He'd promised to take Amy to Paris and Rome for a graduation present if she maintained passing grades. Amy had received two A's and she'd loved the summer in Europe with her father and Rita.

She'd set out to attract Mike Speer with the same kind of stubborn insistence. First she'd made a study of his girlfriends. He seemed to prefer women with long hair, so she'd let hers grow, even when the styles were short. He loved John Ford films, so she'd rented every one she could find and watched them five times apiece. He was interested in sailing, so she'd read everything she could on the subject and then persuaded everyone she knew with a sailboat to take her out until she'd become a competent sailor. At the same time, she'd worn her sexiest outfits. She'd even resorted to sunbathing without a top. All the charms she'd learned worked perfectly on other men but Mike didn't get the message.

Amy blushed as she remembered that night, six years ago, when she'd made up her mind to seduce Mike. They had all agreed to meet for dinner and dancing at a nightclub in New York. Flip and his girlfriend, Amy and her dopey cousin, Norman, and Mike and his latest airline stewardess. Amy wasn't surprised when Mike had called to say he'd be meeting them alone. There'd been some sort of delay in Los Angeles and his date was stuck there for the night. Amy had known better. The telegram she'd sent this morning, inviting Mike's stew to a party at one of the major studios, had been worth every penny. She didn't even have to beg out of her date with her cousin. Amy had been so sure of success, she hadn't invited Norman in the first place.

"Looks like both of us are out in the cold tonight." Mike grinned at Amy as he pulled out her chair. "Do you think you can put up with me for the whole night?"

Amy looked up at him, running her fingers through the hairstyle that had taken three hours to accomplish, and laughed. "The whole night? Is that a threat or a promise?"

Mike laughed. Flip's little sister had an outrageous sense of humor.

Amy did her best to recover her composure. She shouldn't have said that. The remark she'd thought would come out sexy and witty had sounded childish. Thank goodness the waiter was coming to take their drink orders. It would give her time to think of something adult to say.

Perhaps she'd be a little more relaxed if she had a drink. Unfortunately, Amy didn't know what to order. Would they serve her a real drink? She'd die of embarrassment if she had to settle for carbonated grape juice or one of those awful Shirley Temples. Amy decided to go for broke. Flip's girlfriend was having a martini but she'd tried a sip of Rita's once and it tasted like kerosene smelled. The olives were good but there was only one per drink. What could she order?

"I'll have a Glenmorangie, Andrew. Neat." Mike turned to Amy with a question in his eyes.

Suddenly Amy remembered a girl at school going into raptures about the exotic drinks she'd been served on a cruise. "I'd like a piña colada, please."

Mike looked shocked for a second and then he laughed. "Why not? It's New Year's Eve. No drinking the rest of the year, though. You're still a kid."

Amy was so embarrassed she said the first thing that came to her mind. "Open your eyes, Mike. Do I look like a kid?"

Mike laughed and raised his eyebrows. "You sure don't. Sorry, Amy. I guess I miss that freckle-faced kid who used to sit on my lap."

"Don't worry, Mike. I'll be happy to sit on your lap. Just tell me when."

Mike laughed and Amy smiled radiantly. That was more like it. At least he seemed to be enjoying her wisecracks. Now if she could only get him to notice the new dress she was wearing. . . .

When the drinks came, Amy took a good healthy sip of hers. Her knees were shaking and she was more nervous than she'd ever been before in her life. She was surprised to find that the drink tasted just like pineapple fruit punch. Perhaps the waiter thought she was too young and had left out the liquor.

By the time dinner was over, Amy had gone through two more piña coladas and she knew the waiter had been fooled. Her knees had stopped trembling and now she couldn't feel her legs at all. She guessed that was preferable—she certainly wasn't nervous anymore.

"Amy?" Amy looked up with a start. Mike was pulling out her chair. He must have asked her to dance. She put on her best smile and hoped her legs wouldn't fail her now. Everything worked just fine as they got out on the dance floor. Mike held her close but not as closely as some of the other couples. He was still treating her like a kid.

Amy cuddled up as close as she dared and shut her eyes. That didn't work at all. With her eyes closed, she felt dizzy and it wasn't a pleasant sensation.

"Are you feeling all right, Amy?"

"Oh, yes! I'm fine." Amy gazed up into Mike's eyes. He looked genuinely concerned as he led her off the dance floor. Amy could have died from embarrassment. Now he'd think she was just a kid who couldn't handle a couple of drinks. If she was going to make a move at all, the time was now.

"Mike?"

"Yes, Amy."

"Let's go to bed, Mike."

Mike did a double-take and then he grinned. Naturally Amy hadn't meant what he'd thought at first. She'd be really embarrassed if she knew exactly what she said.

"Sure, Amy." Mike took her arm. "I'll get the car and take you home. You look a little tired."

"No, that's not what I mean." Amy shook her head. "I want both of us to go to bed."

"Amy!" Mike looked shocked. "Look, honey, I'm flattered but . . . well . . . I respect you too much for something like that. You're my best friend's baby sister and I just couldn't do that to Flip!"

"I don't want you to do it to Flip! I want you to do it to *me!*"

Mike threw back his head and laughed. Then he pulled her close and kissed her on the forehead.

"You're a tease, Amy! For a minute there, I thought you were serious but I should have known better. You've always had a great sense of humor!"

Amy laughed along with Mike but she felt sick inside. He thought she was teasing. She guessed it was better than being rejected outright, but it still hurt.

"Okay, I'm recovered." Amy stood up and flashed her brightest smile. "If you won't take me to bed, let's go back on the dance floor and I'll let you step on my toes some more."

Amy stared up at the darkness and sighed. It was hell being the only woman in the world that Mike Speer respected! Of course, Amy hadn't given up after that New Year's Eve. There was the summer, Flip's last one at home before enlisting in the Navy. Amy had tried every trick in the book to get Mike to notice her. And here she was, at twenty-three, still trying, though of course she wasn't using childish tricks anymore. The pangs of unrequited love, the subject of almost every country and western song. It would have been funny if it hadn't been so painful.

There were times, like tonight, when working with Mike was almost too much to bear. After the tryouts, Amy had rushed out to find him. Perhaps it wasn't too late for that hamburger. Then she'd talked to Stan at the Dome Room bar. One peek at Mike's table and she'd known exactly what was happening. Amy had gone home alone.

Amy stared up at the ceiling and thought about Valerie Jeffries, well over forty and definitely sophisticated. Amy fell asleep wondering whether she should visit the cosmetologist at the Speer Palace Beauty Shop tomorrow for an older-looking hairstyle.

Breakfast had been delicious. Mike finished the last of his coffee and headed back to the floor to make an early morning check on the action at the tables.

A bank of electronic slots flanked the snack bar entrance and Mike strolled over. There were nickel, dime, and quarter machines. When the state-of-the-art slots were first manufactured, they'd come with a button instead of a handle. People had avoided them with a passion. Slot players liked the action of pulling the handle. They mistakenly felt it gave them some control over the game. Now even the electronic slots had handles and sound effects that simulated the spinning wheels. Mike stopped to watch a man playing a quarter machine. There was something about him that wasn't quite right.

Seasoned casino employees learned to spot "zoo behavior." If a monkey happened to be scratching his head when someone threw him a peanut, the monkey would go on scratching indefinitely, trying to get another. All it took was once and the animal was hooked. Hard core slot machine players were the same way.

Mike thought of the middle-aged lady who came in every Sunday to play her favorite machine. She never failed to pat the machine before she pulled the handle. Once she'd hit a jackpot that way and she'd been trying for the second jackpot ever since. Another regular was a talker. He sweet-talked the machine before every pull. There were other gamblers who swore they won jackpots by feeding in coins at a certain rhythm or in a complicated sequence.

This man had his own peculiar habit, one that Mike

had never seen before. He kept his left hand pressed tightly to the side of the machine while he pulled the handle with his right. Two cherries came up on the display and six quarters skittered into the tray beneath the machine. One of them bounced out onto the floor. The man saw it fall but he didn't bother to pick it up. That was even more curious. Most gamblers believed that money dropped on the floor brought bad luck.

Mike approached the man and tapped him gently on the shoulder. The man whirled around looking guilty as hell. "Excuse me, sir." Mike smiled and pointed to the quarter on the floor. "I think that's your money under the machine."

"Oh, yeah. I guess it is." The man gave a nervous smile. "Thanks, buddy."

Mike stepped back as the man bent down to pick up the quarter. Even though it put him in an awkward position, the man kept his left hand glued to the side of the machine. His sleeve pulled up just far enough for Mike to catch a glimpse of a wire running up the inside of his arm. Mike didn't waste any time. He walked quickly to the aisle and pressed the beeper in his pocket. In seconds two plain-clothes security men materialized at his side.

"I think we've got him." Mike spoke softly. "Wait until he hits and then take him in."

One security guard sat down at the slot on the end and plunked two quarters in the machine. The other took up a position farther down. Mike stood behind a girl with thick glasses who was playing the nickel poker machines.

A moment later bells began to ring. The man had hit a thirty-thousand-dollar progressive jackpot. Before he had time to move a muscle, Mike's security guards flanked him. "Please come with us, sir. We have to issue a check for a payoff this large."

The man looked like he was about to protest but Mike's men were pros. They hustled him out before he had a chance to say a word. The girl at the poker machine turned to Mike with a frown. "What a dummy! He didn't even play it off. Sometimes those things hit twice in a row."

"His loss, your gain." Mike laughed and handed her a roll of quarters. He could afford to be generous. Before the day was over, every one of those quarters would wind up inside a Speer Palace machine.

"Hey, thanks!" The girl gave him a big smile. "You want a cut if I win?"

"It's all yours." Mike gave her a smile before he hurried toward the security office. "I've already had my luck for the morning."

The slot machine cheater was sticking to his story. Mike thought it sounded like the truth. Four different people had questioned him and now Mike sat behind the desk, facing the perspiring man. "All right, Mr. Turner. Tell me exactly what happened."

Ralph Turner grabbed the cup of coffee Mike pushed across the desk and gulped it. He was scared and it showed. "It's just like I told those other guys. I met a man in a bar and he gave me this thing. He was some kind of electronic nut, out here for a convention or something. He showed me how to use it and made me promise to use it only at the Speer Palace and get rid of it after I'd hit."

"How many times did you use this device, Mr. Turner?"

"Twice. Once yesterday afternoon and then just a

couple of minutes ago. I . . . I got greedy. I had reservations to fly out of here this morning and I thought it couldn't hurt to try it one more time. . . ."

"What happened to the jackpot you won?"

"That was the good part. He said I could keep it. He didn't want the money. He just wanted to get even with the Speer Palace. He said he'd lost a bundle in here the other night. I . . . I didn't even cash the check from the other jackpot. It's still in my wallet!"

Ten minutes later Mike had arranged for an expert at M.I.T. to fly out. Dr. Rauch was sure he could prevent the same thing from working again if he could examine the device. The slot machine run was over but Mike's worst fears were confirmed.

Amy sat across the room from Flip and Mike, listening to the report of the slot machine cheater. Mike looked tired and she felt a pang of sympathy until she remembered that Valerie Jeffries had helped wear him out.

"I think I'll pay a little visit to Claudio Petrelli. If this thing is mob-related, he'll know about it."

"Petrelli?" Flip's face turned white. "Are you sure that's a good idea, Mike? Petrelli's in Chicago. He might not know anything about Jersey."

"Claudio's always kept his ear to the ground. I'll just mention it to him."

Flip nodded but Mike noticed that he winced as he took a sip of his coffee. Mike could understand why Flip was so reluctant to get involved with the Petrelli family. Claudio Petrelli was a powerful man and he could be ruthless if the occasion demanded it. Mike knew how important it was to steer clear of any Mafia involvement but Claudio was more than the don of the

Chicago area, he was a longtime family friend and his father's former partner. When Nicholas came back from the war he had founded Speer International, and Claudio another kind of empire. It was probably best not to delve too deeply into Claudio's business, but Mike knew he could count on him for some straight answers.

"How about Jack Humphries?" Amy spoke up. "If Petrelli can't help, maybe Jack could work on it."

"Jack Humphries?" Mike looked at Flip and grinned. "That's a great idea, Amy. I'll get him here today."

Mike was in good spirits as he took a taxi to the airport and secured a seat on the first flight out to Chicago. Amy had managed to locate Jack and he was eager to discuss a job at the Speer Palace.

"Good afternoon, Mr. Speer." A smiling stewardess took Mike's boarding pass and ushered him to his seat in the first-class section. Mike put his briefcase under the seat and closed his eyes, barely hearing the low hum of conversation as the other passengers were seated. By the time the plane taxied down the runway, Mike was lost in thought, remembering Thorton Military Academy and the day that he and Flip had met their tough cadet leader.

3

IT WAS SEPTEMBER of 1968 and the airport was filled with college students going back to school. Most of the boys had beards and long hair. They wore jeans and T-shirts, the standard hippie look. Mike barely glanced at them. It was the girls that made 1968 a good year. Some wore Indian-print cotton dresses that swept to the floor but Mike was much more interested in the coeds who had opted for miniskirts. The feast of bare, golden-tanned thighs took his breath away and, even better, the "no-bra" look was definitely in.

Mike knew he was staring but he couldn't help it. One little blonde in a beaded leather vest and the shortest miniskirt Mike had ever seen looked just like Goldie Hawn on *Laugh-In.* Mike stretched up to his full five feet seven inches and tried to look older as he walked past her. He wished he were going away to college instead of a dumb military academy but his father had insisted. Thorton Academy was the finest in the country and Nicholas Spiros wanted only the best for his eleven-year-old son.

The cute blonde bent over to adjust her sandal and Mike was treated to a delightful view. At the same instant, a skinny, brown-haired boy walking a few paces ahead of Mike stopped abruptly to read the signs to the baggage terminal. Mike, still staring at the blonde's incredible bottom, collided with him squarely.

"Sorry about that. Here, let me help." Mike knelt down to pick up some things that had fallen out of the boy's duffel bag. The other boy turned to look and both boys stared as the blonde took time to adjust her other sandal. They sighed in unison as she straightened up and walked away.

"I think you did me a favor." The brown-haired boy grinned at Mike. "I would have missed the view if you hadn't bumped into me."

"Hey. What's this?" Mike picked up a silver flask.

"It's supposed to hold cologne but I filled it with Scotch. One of my friends told me it's the only way to survive Thorton."

"Thorton Military Academy? That's where I'm going! My name's Mike Speer."

"I'm Philip Warner but my friends call me Flip." The two boys shook hands and grinned, then headed for the baggage terminal.

A gray-haired man holding a red sign stood by the door to the baggage terminal. "Thorton Military Academy? Right over here, boys!"

By the time Flip and Mike had collected their baggage and were seated in the dark-blue station wagon that belonged to Thorton Military Academy, they were fast friends. Mike confessed that he hadn't thought to bring booze but he did have twelve back issues of *Playboy* in his suitcase. Flip thought they ought to be worth as much as the booze.

Thorton Academy was impressive with its ivy-covered buildings and parade ground. Since more than a hundred new plebes had arrived during the past two days, it was easy working out a switch so Mike and Flip could be roommates. All it took was the pound of peanut butter fudge that the Warner's cook had made and Mike's Miss January centerfold as a bribe. In a matter of minutes the two boys found themselves sharing the end room on the third floor of Rice Hall. The food that night was good and the third floor was filled with congenial boys. By the time taps sounded for lights out, both Mike and Flip began to think that they might enjoy Thorton.

That was before they met their squad leader, Jack Humphries. Humphries woke them up at six for inspection. He seemed to be especially tough on Flip and Mike, even though their room was much neater than any of the rest on the third floor. All through the day Flip and Mike collected demerits. Their socks weren't rolled up correctly, their posture was improper at dinner, their uniforms were sloppy. Most of the new boys got demerits, but Mike and Flip had collected three times as many as the rest. Their squad leader seemed to hate them.

Mike came back to his room on the fifth day of classes to find Flip nursing a bloody nose.

"Jesus, Flip! What happened?"

"It's that creep, Humphries. He said my hair was too long so he made me wear a scarf over my head like a girl." Flip leaned his head back and pinched the bridge of his nose. Even though he sounded a bit like Donald Duck that way, Mike was too concerned to crack a smile.

"You got a bloody nose from a scarf?"

"Naw, Kowalski grabbed me before sixth period history, so I hit him. He hit me back and that's how I got the bloody nose. I think it's stopped now."

"You hit Kowalski?" Mike winced. The big cadet outweighed Flip by at least fifty pounds.

"What else could I do? If I'd let him kiss me, all the other guys would have tried it, too."

Repressing a smile, Mike sighed. "Okay, Flip. I'll walk you to class early on Monday and deck Kowalski if he tries anything."

"Thanks, Mike, but won't you be late for your class?"

"Don't worry about that, Flip. I've already been on report for so long, I'll never get off. Throw me that towel. I'll run some cold water on it."

Mike walked down the hall to the latrine and rinsed out the towel. Then he took a piece of paper toweling and cleaned out the sink. Policing the latrine was their duty this week and both he and Flip could hardly wait to be assigned to something else. Humphries was running his inspection tonight and tomorrow he'd give the new duty assignments.

When Mike got back, Flip was staring morosely out the window at the parade ground below where a platoon of upper-classmen was drilling for Sunday's parade.

"You'd better snap to, Flip. Ten minutes to chow time."

"Go on without me, Mike. I'm not hungry."

"No way." Mike went over and hoisted Flip to his feet. "If you don't show up, Kowalski'll think he's got you running scared."

Flip shrugged. "Then he'll be right. I *am* running scared. I punched him as hard as I could and he didn't even blink. That guy's an ox!"

"The bigger they are, the harder they fall, that's what

my dad always says. Come on. I'll run interference for you tonight and this weekend I'll teach you to box. I've got two pairs of gloves in my trunk."

"Really? Thanks, Mike!" Mike grinned as Flip jumped up and got into his uniform. All he needed was a little self-confidence.

Two hours later Flip and Mike were waiting in the spotless latrine.

"Ten-hut!" Humphries banged open the door while Mike and Flip stood stiffly at attention. He glared at the two boys and Mike could almost feel Flip's nervousness. Jack Humphries was big and his bulging muscles and stocky frame looked like that of a professional wrestler. He had carrot-colored hair and freckles but no one had ever dreamed of calling him "Red." The plebes stuck to "sir" as in "Yes, sir" and "No, sir."

"Well, let's see what kind of job you two fuck-ups did." Jack favored them with a chilling grin and pulled on white gloves. Mike and Flip stared straight ahead as he ran his hand under the bottom of the sink.

"Sink, clean! Mirrors, clean! Fixtures, clean! Door, clean! Floor . . . how about this floor, fuck-ups? It doesn't look clean to me." They watched in consternation as their squad leader unzipped his pants . . . pulled it out . . . and pissed his way across the gleaming, white tiled floor.

"Warner and Speer? You're on report! No town privileges until this latrine passes my inspection. Now . . . clean it up!"

Jack turned and barged out through the door, while the boys looked at each other helplessly. A full minute of silence passed before Mike was able to hiss, "That bastard!"

"What do we do now?" Flip looked down at the puddle of urine on the floor and swallowed hard.

Mike sighed. "We clean it up. And then we do some serious thinking about how we can get even with that son-of-a-bitch."

The next morning an upperclassman took pity on them, explaining that Jack never picked on anyone who didn't have leadership potential. Jack must be really impressed with Mike and Flip or he wouldn't be putting this much effort into making them miserable.

Mike and Flip decided there was something definitely perverse about the Thorton Academy system but there wasn't much they could do about it. They learned that no plebe had ever gotten the best of Jack Humphries but they vowed to be the first. A month passed in misery. Mike and Flip were continually on report for minor infractions of the rules. That meant they had no town privileges. The other boys in Rice Hall went into town every weekend and Mike and Flip began to do a slow burn as they heard about the thick chocolate milkshakes at the town drugstore, the gorgeous town girls, and the discount Thorton cadets received at the first-run movie theater.

On the first weekend the local movie theater had shown *Planet of the Apes* and they were the only boys in Rice Hall who hadn't seen it. The next two weekends they had missed *Oliver!* and *Rosemary's Baby*. Last weekend they had stayed in their rooms while all the other plebes went to see Barbra Streisand's *Funny Girl*. This week the town theater was showing *2001: A Space Odyssey*. Flip swore he'd strangle Humphries with his bare hands if he didn't get to see it.

Every Saturday morning the plebes lined up on the

parade ground for the ritual of assigning duty for the coming week. On the Saturday of the fourth week, Mike and Flip had known exactly what to expect, another rerun.

Squad Leader Jack Humphries had stood in front of them with a clipboard, barking out orders. Two by two, the plebes had received their duty assignments and were dismissed. Mike and Flip had glanced at each other without hope. There were only two other plebes left.

"Mess duty . . . Reynolds and Simpkins!"

Mike and Flip had stared straight ahead as Reynolds and Simpkins stepped out of rank, turned smartly, and marched away. There was only one duty left.

"Latrine duty . . . Speer and Warner!" Jack Humphries had glowered at them. "You two are going to keep doing it until you get it right. I want a clean floor!"

Flip and Mike had stepped out, turned smartly, and marched back to Rice Hall, knowing better than to complain. The faculty never interfered in what they called "Squad Discipline."

Flip had waited until they got back to their room before he exploded. "That fucker! He's had us on report for a month and we can't even watch television in the recreation room. Do you realize I haven't seen *Mission: Impossible* or *Get Smart* since I've been here? I'm gonna kill him! I swear I'm gonna kill him!"

Flip had frowned so hard his brown eyebrows almost met in the center. Mike had patted him on the shoulder to calm him down. "Relax, Flip. The package I ordered from that pharmaceutical catalog came this morning. We're all set."

"Let me see." Flip had held out his hand and Mike

had poured out a couple of the capsules. They'd looked perfectly innocent, almost like the gelatin capsules that girls took to make their fingernails grow.

"Are you sure this'll work?"

"Positive. Who did you tell?"

"Andy Roche—his older brother is Jack's roommate. I told Andy that there's a new kind of V.D. going around. You know you've got it when your piss turns blue and the only cure is a series of shots you know where. Then I swore Andy to secrecy and that means it's all over Thorton by now."

Flip and Mike had grinned at each other. They were in good spirits for the first time in a month. The trap was baited and all they had to do was sneak into Jack's room on Friday and slip a couple of the pills into his bottle of rye whiskey. Jack always took a big swig after dinner and twenty minutes later he came down to inspect the latrine.

The week passed slowly but, at last, it was Friday. Flip watched the hall while Mike sneaked into Jack's room. They used four pills, just to be on the safe side. A few minutes later they were in line at the mess hall, looking innocent as they stuffed down hamburger dinners and two pieces of apple pie à la mode apiece.

Skip Jackson, one of the upperclassmen, strolled past their table. He stopped to snag a French fry off Mike's plate. "Hey, plebes, just a word to the wise. Be careful if you go to town tonight. I heard there's a new kind of V.D. going around. Your piss turns blue. Five of our guys got it already."

Flip managed to look shocked while Mike nodded gravely. By the time their meal was over, three other upperclassmen had mentioned the new form of V.D. Flip's rumor had definitely made the rounds. An hour later Flip and Mike stood stiffly at attention while Jack inspected the latrine.

"Sink . . . clean! Mirrors . . . clean! Fixtures . . . clean! Doors . . . clean! Floor . . . I don't know about this floor, plebes. It doesn't look clean to me!"

This time Jack grinned openly as he unzipped his pants. Flip sneaked a look at Mike but Mike was facing straight ahead, his face impassive. Jack aimed and let go. Then he gave a yelp as he polluted the white tiled floor with blue piss.

There was a moment of startled silence as Jack stared down at the telltale puddle of blue. He didn't even bother telling Mike and Flip to clean it up. He just zipped up his pants and ran for the phone to call his girl in town.

The next morning Mike and Flip lined up on the parade ground with the other plebes. Humphries paced in front of them, clipboard in his hand. Both Mike and Flip were nervous. They knew the axe was going to fall and they stood stiffly at attention while he barked out the orders. Within minutes there were only four plebes left. It looked as if Mike and Flip were going to draw latrine duty again. "Latrine duty . . . Darnell and Kowalski!"

Mike and Flip raised eyebrows in astonishment as Darnell and Kowalski stepped out of rank, saluted, turned smartly, and marched away. Jack Humphries waited until they were well out of earshot before he continued.

"Speer and Warner? Looks like you've got mess duty this week." Mike and Flip stepped out of rank and saluted but Jack's voice stopped them before they could march away.

"All right, you two fuck-ups. Your little joke was real

cute." Mike and Flip stared straight ahead, expecting to hear that they were on report for the whole year.

"You're the worst smart-asses at Thorton but at least you had the brains to shut up about the whole thing. If I'd heard one word about what happened last night, I'd have broken both your faces. Now tell me exactly how you did it."

Flip held his breath while Mike explained about the pills. Jack Humphries didn't exactly look mad and that was encouraging—unless he was planning on setting them at ease before he killed them. "And that's how, sir!" Mike finished his explanation and saluted smartly.

"At ease!" Jack Humphries looked thoughtful. "I gotta admire guts like that. I could have killed you, you know."

Mike and Flip nodded. They still weren't sure what was going to happen until Jack Humphries started to grin.

"Speer and Warner? You're the only two plebes this year who aren't total wimps. If you got any of those pills left, I figure we could slip 'em to Kowalski."

"Would you care for a cocktail, Mr. Speer?"

The pretty stewardess brought Mike back from the past with a jolt. She looked exactly like Brooke Shields, pretty enough to work at the Speer Palace.

"Just a cup of coffee, please. No cream, no sugar."

Mike grinned as the stewardess walked away, the skirt of her blue uniform swishing provocatively.

"Ladies and gentlemen, Captain Lewis has turned off the No Smoking sign. We may be experiencing slight turbulence and we suggest that you keep your seatbelt buckled while you are in your seat for optimum comfort. This afternoon we'll be flying at fourteen thousand feet, landing in Chicago at approximately one-fifteen, Central Standard Time. Please watch the cabin attendant nearest you for a demonstration of our safety procedures."

An attractive redhead took her place in the center aisle, smiling her best I'm-here-to-help-you smile. Mike watched her buckle an unattached seatbelt and put on an oxygen mask. He grinned as she picked up a seat cushion and showed how it could double as a flotation device. The largest body of water they'd be flying over was Claudio Petrelli's swimming pool and it would be one hell of a long shot if they crash-landed there. This whole trip was a long shot. Claudio might not know anything.

After the stewardess finished her demonstration, Mike loosened his seatbelt and tipped his seat back all the way. He shut his eyes and tried to organize the questions he needed to ask Claudio, but he was asleep by the time the Brooke Shields look-alike came back with his coffee.

4

GINA DANELLO WAS on her eighteenth lap. She was wearing a new Speedo racing suit that added only two ounces to her one hundred and three pounds. Gina had fallen in love with the suit when she'd tried it on. The wide red and white diagonal stripes made her look taller than her petite five feet three, and her Uncle Claudio's joke about his niece who looked like a barber pole hadn't fazed her in the slightest.

Gina's short black hair was tucked up into a white swimming cap and an official waterproof timing clock sat at the edge of the pool, ticking off the seconds as her tanned arms cut the clear water in the steady rhythm that made up her successful racing style. Everyone commented on Gina's racing rhythm. It was just fast enough to push her to the limit of her strength but it never exhausted her. Only Amy Warner knew the secret of Gina's rhythm. They had been roommates at Fairview School ten years ago, when Gina had gone out for the swimming team. Mrs. Butler, the Fairview athletic coach, was satisfied with Gina's style but her rhythm was wrong. Gina worked with her coach for a month but nothing they tried seemed to help. Gina was almost ready to give up competitive swimming until Amy came into the picture.

Amy had convinced Gina to put off her decision for another week. The next afternoon she had cut class to watch Gina practice. After a few minutes she had left, calling out to Gina to meet her in their room after the session.

"I timed you and I've got the perfect solution." Amy had been grinning as Gina came in the door. "It takes you sixteen strokes to get to the far end of the lane. Then you turn and go back again, right?"

"Right. Hold on a second. I've got to hang this stuff up."

Amy had followed Gina into the bathroom and watched as she draped her bathing suit over the showerhead.

"Sixteen strokes is One Potato twice. You say it twice for every lap you swim, get it?"

"One Potato? What's that?"

Amy had laughed. "It's a kid's game my dad used to play with me. The rhythm's really catchy. *One potato, two potato, three potato, four. Five potato, six potato, seven potato, more."*

Gina remembered thinking that Amy had been out in the sun for too long but her roommate was insistent. Amy had forced Gina to repeat the rhyme right there in the bathroom until she got the rhythm right.

"Fine!" Amy had grinned. "Now say it in your head when you swim and you'll win the championship."

Gina had been dubious but Amy was a good friend and, at this point, it couldn't hurt to try her suggestion. The next day Gina had One Potatoed at practice and her coach had been delighted. Gina figured she had One Potatoed about a million times during practice. Amy had been right. She'd gone on to win the cup in swimming at Fairview.

The phone on the patio rang but Gina didn't lose her rhythm. Either Uncle Claudio or the answer phone would pick it up. She knew the call couldn't be for her. Gina made a point never to give out her home number. It was best not to advertise that she was Claudio Petrelli's niece.

Gina completed her turn and headed for the shallow end of her uncle's Olympic-sized swimming pool. Uncle Claudio seemed proud of her accomplishments. Gina's Fairview trophy stood in a case in the living room and he'd done everything he could to make her feel that she was part of his family. It was too bad Aunt Dixie didn't feel that way. Claudio's wife had made no secret of her disapproval when Gina had come to live with them. Dixie felt Claudio's only loyalty should be to his own son, Vince.

Aunt Dixie and Vince had left the house over an hour ago. Gina supposed they'd gone shopping. Dixie's chief pleasure in life seemed to be spending money on her son. Vince had been the only high school junior in Chicago with a new Jaguar. He had cracked it up in his senior year but Dixie had replaced it with a newer model. Vince was on his fifth Jaguar now. Dixie always made sure her son had everything he wanted, from designer clothes to the best in stereo equipment.

Gina hated Vince, mostly because he was such a lousy son to Uncle Claudio. Of course Vince treated his father with respect when they were face-to-face but Gina had overheard plenty when Uncle Claudio wasn't around. Neither Vince nor Dixie had any real respect. Only her feeling for her uncle brought Gina to Chicago every summer vacation. Claudio Petrelli might be the don of the Chicago area but he wasn't a bit frightening to Gina. She loved him with all her heart.

Gina was finishing her twenty-second lap when she heard Vince's Jaguar roar up the driveway. It was time to make herself scarce. She jumped out of the water, grabbed her yellow terry-cloth bathrobe, and slipped in through the patio doors. She raced up the circular staircase, two steps at a time, and ran down the hall to her room. She didn't breathe easy again until she was inside with the door locked securely behind her.

Perhaps it was only her imagination, but Gina was afraid of Vince. Her cousin hadn't paid much attention to her until this summer. Now, when Vince looked at her, there was something in his eyes that made Gina shiver.

Gina went into her bathroom and stripped off her suit. She tried to look as unattractive and dowdy as she could whenever she was around Vince. Fifteen minutes later, dressed in tan pull-on slacks and a polo shirt, Gina went downstairs. It was time to fix lunch. The maid was taking her summer vacation and Dixie avoided the kitchen like the plague. Gina had volunteered to take over the kitchen duties. Actually, she didn't mind. It was fun to try out new recipes for Uncle Claudio and time in the kitchen got her away from Dixie and Vince.

Gina was standing at the kitchen sink, washing lettuce for a seafood salad, when a taxi pulled up the circular driveway. An attractive man, who looked vaguely familiar, got out and paid the driver. A moment later he disappeared around the corner of the house and headed for the private entrance to her uncle's office. Gina had learned to pay no attention to the comings and goings of her uncle's business associates but this time she was intrigued.

When the salad was finished, Gina fixed two attractive plates for Dixie and Vince. Then she took a deep breath and headed for the patio.

"Here's lunch, Aunt Dixie." Gina put the tray down on the patio table. Dixie was stretched out on a chaise longue under the shade of the awning. Since her hair was a different shade of red than it had been yesterday, Gina deduced she'd come from the beauty salon. Dixie's true hair color was a mousy brown but she told everyone it was natural auburn.

"Thank you, dear." Dixie sat up and slipped a matching beach jacket over her designer shorts and halter. Gina's aunt was well past fifty but she refused to admit it, dieting constantly and going to an exclusive figure salon for daily workouts. Gina remembered the trips Dixie had taken to "European health spas" and how well her aunt had looked when she'd returned. Gina had thought it was all due to diet and exercise until the day she'd overheard Dixie talking to a friend about her doctor's marvelous face-lifts and tummy tucks.

Gina arranged the silverware and put a linen napkin by both plates. Dixie favored her with a smile as she sat down. "You really didn't have to go to all this trouble, dear. Your uncle wants you to relax on your vacation."

"It's no trouble, Aunt Dixie. I like to cook."

"Vince?" Dixie raised her voice to a pitch that would carry across the huge swimming pool. "Come here, honey. Gina's fixed us lunch." Then she got up and headed toward the house. "I'll just go powder my nose and then we'll eat."

Vince climbed off the diving board where he'd been sunning himself and stretched. The muscles he'd developed from high school weight-lifting were still apparent and he was in the habit of flexing them whenever anyone was watching. Gina noticed that he'd gained a few pounds since last summer and she was sure the thickness around her cousin's waist was due to expensive restaurants and hard drinking.

"It's hotter than hell out here, right, Gina?" Vince picked up a towel and wiped his face. He draped it around his thick shoulders and grinned at her. Women found Vince's darkly Italian looks attractive, as he'd often reminded Gina. His deeply tanned body glistened with sweat as he walked over, and Gina averted her eyes. Vince had never affected her one way or the other before and Gina couldn't understand why she was so nervous around him this summer; perhaps because he kept staring at her.

"What's the matter, Gina?" Vince moved so close that the dark hair on his broad chest almost touched her, but she stood her ground. His long arm shot out and he grabbed her around the waist. "There's only two plates. You think you're too good to eat with us?"

"Of course not!" Gina tried to move away but Vince pulled her closer, his arm like a steel band. "I . . . I'm just not hungry, that's all."

"I don't like skinny women, Gina. I get bruises from their hip bones."

"Gina, dear?" Dixie opened the patio door and Vince dropped his arm. "We're all out of margaritas and I'm hopeless at mixing drinks. Do you suppose you could . . ."

"Of course, Aunt Dixie." Gina jumped at the chance to get away. "I'll mix up a pitcher and be right back."

"Need some help?" Vince made a move toward the door.

"No! You'd better start on your salad before it gets cold . . . I . . . I mean hot."

Gina raced off to the kitchen and mixed the margaritas with shaking hands. Just as soon as she'd poured the drinks she hurried to her room.

Gina couldn't shake the feeling that Vince could see right through her clothes. She felt defiled in some vague, unpleasant way and she knew she'd wake with a nightmare tonight. It was Vince's eyes that made her shudder. They were bright, too bright, and there was something in their depths. Gina threw the dead bolt she had installed on her bedroom door. She didn't dare to think of what might happen if Vince ever caught her in the house alone.

Mike sat on the leather couch in Claudio's office. He'd seen Claudio briefly at his father's funeral but had never visited the don in his home before.

"The last time we talked was nine years ago, at your twenty-first birthday party. Right, Michael?"

Mike nodded. "That's right. We weren't sure you were coming until the limo drove up the driveway. Dad said no celebration would be complete without my Italian godfather."

Claudio laughed, and as the deep lines disappeared from his face he looked for a brief moment like the powerful man in his father's photographs. Claudio was still a handsome man with a full head of silver hair and deep penetrating eyes. Mike remembered how terrified he'd been as a child when he'd first heard Claudio's gruff voice, but it hadn't taken him long to realize that the big Italian could be gentle and loving. Mike had looked forward to his godfather's infrequent visits to their ranch in Arizona and the wonderful presents he brought. On one of his early birthdays Claudio had arrived with a remote-control plane and they had spent the whole day out in the yard making it swoop and dive. There were still traces of the jovial man Mike remembered from family occasions in the past, but now there were dark circles under Claudio's eyes and, even though he appeared delighted to see his godson again, Mike could sense that something was worrying the older man.

"Well, Michael?" Claudio removed the cork from a bottle of Chianti Classico and poured a glass for each of them. "I know you didn't come all this way just to pay your respects. What's wrong?"

Mike took a sip of the wine and began to talk. He hated to bother Claudio but he needed answers and he knew he could depend on his godfather to be honest with him. Mike's wine sat untouched on the table as he outlined the history of the Speer Palace.

When he had finished, Claudio leaned back and sighed deeply. "You know how I felt about your father, Michael. We had our differences but we had respect for each other."

"I know that, Uncle Claudio." Mike nodded. He remembered the affection between Nicholas and Claudio. They had met in America in the thirties, two immigrants from different countries helping each other to survive in their adopted land.

"If I'd wanted to close down the Speer Palace, you wouldn't have opened your doors in the first place. You forget I'm a Sicilian. We believe in direct action. Your enemy is more subtle, a man without balls. Probably a Greek."

Mike laughed. Claudio always managed to get the needle in when it came to Greeks and Sicilians. "So what should I do, Uncle Claudio?"

"I'll keep my ears open, Michael." Claudio frowned

slightly. "I have contacts in Jersey. Just remember that the Petrellis would never hurt you. It pains me to say this about a Greek, but you're my godson and that makes you family."

"How's Dixie, Uncle Claudio? And Vince?"

Claudio set down his wineglass and sighed deeply. For a moment Mike wished he hadn't asked about Claudio's family but convention demanded it.

"Dixie." Claudio shook his head. "She wants to fly south for the winter. Doesn't like it in Chicago anymore. She's got her eye on a place in Palm Springs where the rich old *segaiuoli* go to play golf. She also says I should retire and turn everything over to Vince."

Mike wisely kept his silence. An outsider, even one who was practically a member of the family, never interfered between an Italian father and his son.

"Enough about that." Claudio dismissed his son with a wave of his hand. "Tell me about the place, Michael. Eighteen hundred rooms, right? And you're getting good convention business?" Mike nodded. It didn't surprise him that Claudio knew about his operation. The Petrellis kept on top of things.

"National Optometrists this week and another two booked for next week."

"Not enough." Claudio shook his head. "How about a tournament? A two grand buy-in for blackjack, winner's purse, the sort of thing the Sahara does."

"We're planning one for the January slump . . . if I'm still in business by then."

"You will be." Claudio leaned forward and stared straight into Mike's eyes. "Anybody who takes on the Speer Palace takes on the Petrellis, too. Now, go back and run your business, Michael. And don't be such a stranger."

Claudio stood up. The interview was over. Mike felt a great weight drop from his shoulders as he got back into the taxi and headed for the airport. Most men would have relaxed completely after such a promise but Mike believed in hedging his bets. There was a flight leaving for New York in half an hour and if everything went well he could meet Jack in New York and still be back at the Speer Palace in time for his dinner date with Amy.

Amy called in Lottie Perkins, the last of the six cocktail waitresses, and smiled to put the pretty red-head at ease.

"This'll just take a minute, Lottie. I have a message for you from Mr. Speer. He wants you to join him for dinner tonight. Eight o'clock at the Dome Room."

"Oh, thank you, Miss Warner! I'll be there."

Lottie's face lit up in a smile that was every bit as ecstatic as the five other waitresses. Amy gave a bemused grin as the girl rushed back to her duties. Mike should approve of the way she'd handled this situation. All six waitresses would arrive at the Dome Room at eight o'clock. Since the money in the pool was to go to the first waitress Mike dated, it would be a six-way tie and all six waitresses would get their own money back.

Amy swiveled her chair to look out the window. A group of guests were out in the midday sun, enjoying the pool area. A table of older women sat under the cabana, watching a deeply tanned young man perform on the diving board.

The young man was handsome enough to be a movie star. His muscles rippled as he climbed the ladder and he stopped on the end of the board to blow a kiss to the group of women below. Then he executed a perfect dive.

The women applauded and the young man's white teeth flashed in a grin as he climbed out of the water. His body was perfectly proportioned, a young Adonis. He dried himself with a towel and went to sit beside one of the older women. She smiled as he slipped his arm around her shoulders and gave her a kiss.

Amy sighed. Perhaps the woman had spent her youth waiting for the man of her dreams and had awakened one morning to find she was alone, and at an age that forced her to pay for handsome companionship.

The older woman lifted her hand to wave and a distinguished-looking man in his fifties hurried toward her. A beautiful young girl accompanied him. There were hugs and kisses all around and Amy laughed out loud as she recognized the group. The older woman wasn't lonely at all. She was Mrs. Donaldson, here with her husband. And the young man who had hugged her was her grandson. He was being married tomorrow right here in the hotel with a huge reception in the Dome Room. Amy's imagination had gotten the best of her again.

Amy's phone rang and she picked it up. It was Mike. His voice sounded tinny and very far away. "Hello, Mike. We've got a bad connection. If you give me your number, I'll call you back."

Static crackled across the line as Mike laughed.

"That's impossible. I'm calling from Pan Am's flight one-five-six. If you look out your window you might be able to see me. I'm meeting Jack at Kennedy in New York and I'll bring him back with me. Call Chef

Sussman, will you, Amy? Tell him there'll be one more at my table tonight. We'll need at least three more Mandarin Burgers."

"Mandarin Burgers?"

"Right. With the oranges, you know. See you in a couple of hours, Amy. The meeting with Claudio went well. I'll tell you all about it when . . ."

There was a loud burst of static and Amy winced. Then a dial tone came on the line. Amy hung up the phone and laughed. Leave it to Mike to call her from a plane, just to order another couple of hamburgers.

Amy went back to work on her personnel schedule. Two more busboys had quit today and the ad in the paper had provided only one applicant. It was becoming more and more difficult to find people willing to work at the Speer Palace. Amy knew Mike would have to be told but it could wait until after dinner. She thought of Mike's Mandarin Burgers and laughed out loud. It was an excellent choice of menu for tonight. After the six waitresses passed the word, no one would be eager for a dinner date with Mike Speer again.

5

Amy had spent the afternoon calling employment agencies. They needed three maids, a relief desk clerk, two bellboys, and four keno runners. Atlantic City claimed to suffer from a high unemployment rate but no one seemed desperate enough to accept a job at the Speer Palace. It was becoming more and more difficult to find new employees. She had just finished juggling the work schedule around again when there was a knock at her door. Amy crossed her fingers, hoping that it wasn't another employee who was giving notice, and opened the door.

"We're back." Mike came in, followed by a tall, muscular man with red hair and freckles. "I pulled this guy off a red-hot case in Queens by promising him a room overlooking the pool and the chance to see you again."

Amy grinned as she recognized Jack Humphries. He'd grown at least a foot taller and put on a hundred pounds since the last time she had seen him, but there was no mistaking those freckles.

"Hi, Jack. I'm glad you're here."

"Amy?" Jack looked as if he couldn't believe his eyes. "I never would have known you. No Band-Aids!"

Amy laughed as Jack lifted her right off her feet in a bear hug. She remembered the July that Jack had visited them. It was the summer of the skateboard. Mike, Flip, and Jack were experts. They rode their decal-covered boards everywhere, while Amy chased along on foot. She'd been going through an awkward stage. Every time she had attempted to ride, she'd skinned her knees. The boys had dubbed her "Scabby" and refused to let her use their boards. Amy hoped none of them would remember that particular nickname.

"Where's Flip, Amy?" Mike's voice was a little sharper than usual and Amy glanced at him over Jack's shoulder. Could he be jealous of the way Jack was holding her?

"Flip called in a couple of minutes ago. He said he had to take care of something but he'll meet us at the Dome Room. I told Chef Sussman there'd be seven more for dinner. You have a date with six cocktail waitresses tonight."

It took Mike a second but then he started to laugh. "Good girl, Amy!"

Amy nodded. "Do you want me to give Jack a tour of the place before dinner?"

"Sure, that's a good . . . no, wait. I'd better do it." Mike changed his mind in midstream. "Come with us, Amy. You can point out anything I miss."

Amy walked down the hall, Jack on one side of her and Mike on the other. She was more than pleased at the way things had turned out. A little rivalry might do a lot to push Mike in the right direction. Amy gave Jack a grateful smile. Now she was doubly pleased that he'd accepted the job at the Speer Palace.

* * *

The man glanced at his watch and shivered. It was growing dark and the wind swept across the bare parking lot, blowing dirt and debris up against the side of the abandoned warehouse. His contact was deliberately late. It was a ploy to make him nervous, and it was working. Under ordinary circumstances, he would have waited for ten minutes and then left, but these weren't ordinary circumstances.

To make matters worse, it was the sort of muggy, overcast day that brought mosquitoes out in whining droves. The man swatted a big one on his arm and rolled up the window. He wished he could start the car and turn on the air-conditioning but his eight-year-old car always overheated when it idled with the air on. Maybe it was time to get a new car. His had been completely overhauled twice and he knew it wouldn't be long before it would be in the shop again but he kept it for sentimental reasons. It had been a gift from his father on his graduation from college.

The inside of the car was a steam bath and his shirt stuck to his back as he shifted in the seat. Dark clouds rolled across the horizon and there was a low rumble of thunder in the distance. The weatherman had predicted only a ten percent chance of showers and that meant that Atlantic City was in for a summer rainstorm tonight. New Jersey weathermen were always wrong. You could make book on it.

A dust-colored sedan whipped around the corner and pulled up next to the warehouse. The driver rolled down the window and beckoned. The man felt a surge of anger. There was no reason why the sedan had to park so far away. It was another tactic to throw him off-balance, to make him run to the sedan like some kind of scared rabbit.

The man grabbed the envelope that was lying on the passenger seat and hurried across the parking lot to the waiting sedan. As he handed over the envelope his heart pounded hard in his chest. He was scared.

"Where's the schedule?"

The man swallowed past the dryness in his throat. "They're changing it tonight and I figured the old one wouldn't do you any good. Everything'll be all set up by tomorrow. I can get it first thing in the morning." The man knew he was overexplaining but he couldn't help it. His nerves were raw and his voice shook a little as he forced out the words.

The driver smiled. It was frightening. Instinctively the man knew it was the same smile he would give to a victim he was about to kill. "You figured wrong. Our friend's going to be disappointed. Maybe he'll have to teach you to take us seriously."

"I'll have it by tomorrow. I promise."

The driver gave a brief nod, the window rolled up, and the sedan squealed forward. The man barely had time to jump out of the way. He watched until it disappeared around the corner and then gave a huge sigh of relief. He knew how dangerous it was to play games with these people. His knees were shaking and he stumbled slightly as he walked back across the asphalt.

The man got into his car and locked both doors. It was a silly precaution but it made him feel better. The simple act of putting his car in gear and driving out of the parking lot restored some of his calm. He'd tried to talk his boss out of going to Chicago but he couldn't push things without admitting that he knew who was behind the sabotage. They'd both be safe as long as

Mike Speer didn't learn that his enemy was the very person he'd gone to for help. The Petrelli family wanted the Speer Palace and they were powerful enough to get it, one way or the other.

Dusk turned to night and the man switched on his lights. The little car slowed as he took the Boardwalk exit and turned onto the strip. Tourists filled the sidewalks, their faces animate under the multicolored flashing lights. The man wished he could lose himself in those carefree, milling crowds with nothing more to worry about than where to eat or which show to see.

When he was first approached by the Petrellis, he'd intended to plead with Mike to knuckle under. Then he'd realized just how smart the Petrellis were. Mike was too attached to the casino to give up without a fight and the Petrellis had a classic way of getting rid of their opposition. Instead, he was appearing to cooperate, but he'd managed to delay critical information. The Petrellis thought they had him over a barrel with their blackmail scheme but the man was stalling for time. There had to be a way out of this mess.

It was past eleven when Amy drove home. She'd left Mike, Flip, and Jack at Mike's table at the Dome Room, reminiscing about their escapades at Thorton Academy. Mike and Jack were drinking unblended Scotch delivered by Lottie, the redheaded waitress, and Flip had his usual vodka.

"Katy?" Amy unlocked her front door and Katy streaked up to brush against Amy's legs.

"I'm beat, Katy." Amy bent down to scratch Katy's head. "I think I'd better go straight to bed."

Katy followed Amy into the bedroom and jumped up

on the bed. She pawed at the covers to arrange them just right, snuggled down with a wide yawn, and closed her eyes.

Amy sighed and went into the bathroom to brush her teeth. When she came out she saw that the calico was draped over the top of her special pillow. That was definitely a no-no.

"Katy?" Amy tried to be stern with the cute little cat. "You know better than that. Find your own pillow."

There was a brief staring match between Amy and Katy. The cat caved in first, throwing Amy a look of injured pride as she backed off the pillow in question and appropriated another, smaller one. Amy gave her a quick, approving pat before she climbed into bed and turned off the light. No one, not even Katy, was permitted to steal Amy's pillow.

Amy turned on her side and hugged her pillow. She knew it was childish to be so attached to an inanimate object but this pillow had been with her for over fifteen years. Filled with the finest Danish goosedown, it had belonged to her mother, and her father had given it to her when she went off to Fairview. Since then Amy's pillow had gone on her European tour, packed carefully in her carry-on luggage. It had been a fixture in five college dorm rooms, spent a year in a sorority house, and survived her affair with Steve in New York City. Amy spent two anxious days every year waiting for it to be cleaned and fluffed by a reputable dry cleaners. Everything else could go—her record collection, her photograph albums, her jewelry—but this pillow was irreplaceable.

The bed jiggled softly as Katy padded over to cuddle up against Amy's arm. Katy gave another big yawn and settled down, purring contentedly. Amy listened to the cat's soft, even breathing for a moment and then she, too, was asleep.

The two men sat in the visitors' parking space for an hour, smoking silently. Finally the last light winked out in the brick apartment building. It was two in the morning and no traffic was moving on the quiet residential street. The driver nodded at his companion and both men got out of the car noiselessly and walked up the sidewalk to the entrance.

The larger man pulled a plastic strip out of his pocket. It took only a moment to open the security door. They walked down the carpeted hallway silently. There was no need for conversation. They were pros.

All was quiet in apartment one-twelve. After listening at the door for a moment, the larger man again used the strip. This door had been double-locked from the inside and it took him longer, almost a full minute, to throw the second tumbler. There was enough light from the street to see the layout of the apartment. The two men had studied the floor plans of this particular apartment, provided in a full-color brochure by the management. It was plan 2A and it rented for seven hundred and forty dollars a month, not including utilities. The master bedroom was down the hall to the left.

The woman was sleeping soundly, curled on her side. The younger man pointed to the cat, who was stretched out beside her, and made a wringing motion with his hands. The larger man, obviously the leader, shook his head. While killing a cat might be a pleasing diversion for his eager companion, it would only complicate matters.

Both men stared down at the sleeping woman. She

moved slightly, stretching in her sleep, and her nightgown pulled down just far enough to reveal the sweetly rounded curve of her breast. Neither man showed any emotion although the same thought occurred to both of them. They knew what would happen if they deviated from their explicit instructions.

After a moment the older man moved. He was much more agile than one would expect for such a large man. The struggle was silent and very brief. It was the easiest assignment he'd ever had.

Amy awoke to a very real nightmare. She opened her mouth to scream and suddenly she was choking and gagging, trying to spit out a wad of cloth. Something came down over her head, a bag of some sort, shutting out the dim light from the window. She struggled as her arms and legs were tied tightly but it was no use. The arms that held her were too strong. Then she was wrapped in something and lifted effortlessly. Muffled footsteps moved through the apartment and out the door. The outside door opened and closed again, and a dog barked in the distance. Then she was shoved onto something soft and upholstered and a car door slammed closed. She felt the car jiggle with the weight of two people in the front seat, the engine started, and there was the vibration of wheels and a driveshaft beneath her. Not a word had been spoken.

The beginnings of panic set in. Amy knew this was not a dream, no matter how much she wished it to be. Where were they taking her? What were they going to do? She knew she didn't dare speculate. The conclusions were too frightening and her fear would render her even more helpless. There must be something she could do to keep from panicking.

Suddenly Amy had it. She remembered seeing a movie about the abduction of a secret agent. He had counted the turns and the intervals between them, then managed to escape and find his way back to civilization for help.

The car backed out of the lot and turned left. Amy could tell by the way her body tilted. She counted the seconds, using the old system her father had taught her to measure the passage of time. One thousand one, one thousand two, one thousand three, one thousand four . . . up to one thousand sixty. That was one minute. The car traveled straight ahead for fifty seconds and then turned left again. They had driven to the end of the block and turned on Brewster. Another two hundred and ten seconds and the driver made a gentle right. The car accelerated faster, faster . . . they were on the freeway. Amy felt her panic setting in again. They could be going forty miles an hour or eighty. She had no way of judging but she counted anyway. When she told the police about this later, it might give them a clue to where she'd been taken. *If* she got a chance to tell the police. . . .

No, she wouldn't think about that. She'd remember the seconds that had elapsed and listen for any unusual sounds. Trains, buses, trucks, airplanes, sirens, anything that might help to identify the area she had traveled through. Now the car was braking, turning off the freeway in a wide curve to the right. It had to be a cloverleaf. They turned almost three hundred and sixty degrees and her back pressed against the seat. The car was tilting upward, climbing onto an overpass. She could hear the traffic below them.

Suddenly Amy knew where she was. There was only one area in Atlantic City that matched this configuration. They were heading south, on the old highway that led out of town. By the time Amy had counted through two more minutes, she was sure she was right. There was very little car traffic on this road, although five big trucks had passed them in the opposite direction. The sedan was buffeted by the backlash of wind and once an air horn had sounded.

Ten minutes later they turned again, right for forty-five seconds and then left, onto a gravel road. Amy bounced painfully on the backseat as the road grew rougher. The car rattled over dips and potholes for three minutes and then stopped.

Amy began to tremble with fear. While the car was moving she had felt relatively safe. Now that the business of driving was over, they could turn their attention to her and whatever they had brought her here to do. The car rocked as the two men got out and slammed the doors. There was a smell of decay in the air. Amy shivered as she heard a rustling sound close to the car. Leaves blowing in the wind? Paper skittering across a parking lot? Rats?

Amy breathed deeply and willed herself to remain calm. Thunder sounded vaguely in the distance, a low ominous rumbling that made Amy's heart pound in her chest. She felt constrained by the bindings on her legs and arms and the hood over her head seemed suddenly suffocating. What were they doing? The waiting was unendurable. She wanted to scream, to strike out against the bonds that held her, but all she could manage was a frightened whimper deep in her throat.

Her hearing seemed magnified. Amy remembered reading that if one sense was lost, the others became more acute. The thunder was growing louder, crashing and booming in the darkness of her prison. The wind had picked up and something struck the side of the car with a ping. Had they left her alone in this unknown place? In some strange way that possibility seemed more ominous than their threatening presence.

Amy's mind seemed to falter and then freeze. She was a mass of screaming nerve endings, a ball of raw terror, trapped in her cocoon of darkness. She had stopped counting when the car pulled over to the shoulder. How much time had passed? Five minutes? An hour? She had no way of knowing.

At last she gathered the courage to move cautiously, to inch herself tightly against the door of the car. The solid metal was comforting against her bare feet. Another shove with her feet and she managed to push herself upright, jamming her back against the side of the car. Her hands were tied behind her back and the blanket had slid down far enough to expose the rope that bound her hands. If she could manage to hook it over the door handle, she might be able to stretch it until it loosened.

The rope chafed at her wrists as she tugged and twisted against the cold metal handle. It seemed to take hours but at last her hands were free. Amy grabbed for the bag that covered her face and tore it off. Her eyes darted frantically, searching the darkness outside, but there was no sign of her captors.

Amy knew they could come back at any minute. Her fingers worked awkwardly at the ropes that bound her legs until she freed them. Then she crawled stiffly into the front seat of the car, not daring to open the door.

Just as Amy had expected, her abductors had taken the keys. She reached out to lock all four doors and felt around under the dash. As a child, she'd watched Flip hot-wire his car whenever he'd misplaced the keys.

Anxious moments passed but finally Amy found the correct wires. With one fluid motion she snapped on the headlights, put the car into gear, and stepped on the gas.

Lightning streaked across the sky and thunder crashed. Amy shivered as she drove over the bumpy gravel road. The headlights illuminated shapes in the distance, the derelict bodies of broken refrigerators and towering heaps of debris. The blackened, burned chassis of old cars lined the ditches and Amy saw moving shapes just out of the range of her headlights. She bit back a scream as one shape darted into the yellow circle of light. It was a rat. The brown, shaggy body was as large as a small dog.

The interior of the car was stifling but Amy didn't dare to open the window. The air was filled with thick smoke and soot sifted down on the windshield. A fire burned in the distance, orange flames licking up against the dark sky.

Was she going in the right direction? There were no road signs, only the gravel road, stretching off into the distance. She felt like the last person left alive in the hellish aftermath of some disaster. Amy held the wheel tightly and concentrated on the road ahead, praying that the car wouldn't break down. The thought of being abandoned here again was more than she could bear.

Gradually the road became wider and smoother. Amy put the car into low gear and crawled up a hill. Tears of relief came to her eyes as she topped the crest and saw the freeway entrance in the distance. It was the most beautiful sight in the world. Other cars. Other people. Safety.

The rain hit the windshield in streaks as Amy pulled onto the freeway. She found the button for the wipers and turned it on the highest speed. She knew she couldn't go home. It wasn't safe. They might come after her again.

Amy turned onto the freeway and merged with the existing traffic. She used her turn signals and moved gradually over into the fast lanes. The car was a midsize Toyota and it was practically new. It was nice of those men to leave her with a reliable Japanese car. A laugh bubbled up out of her throat and it quickly turned into a sob. Amy forced herself to stare at the road and not give way to any emotion. It was a good thing she had learned to drive a stick shift in drivers' education. A man on her right tapped his horn. Amy smiled and let him in ahead of her. She always tried to be courteous on the road. It was one of the things they'd taught her in school.

Amy drove automatically, windshield wipers clicking against the glass. The traffic thickened and she moved over one lane to the right. The freeway was pretty at night. The exit for the Boardwalk was coming up on her right. Amy moved over another lane and then another, when traffic permitted. She made the turnoff perfectly and slowed as she came down the ramp. Casino lights glittered in the darkness and the rain made everything look new.

Amy didn't even consider her destination until she pulled into her parking spot at the Speer Palace. She got out of the car and wrapped the blanket tightly around her. The pavement was cold against her bare feet. A Lincoln Continental pulled into the garage and passed her. Amy didn't notice as the couple in the car stared at her strange outfit She walked to the bank of elevators and got into Mike's private car, punching out the code that would take her up to his suite. She was functioning purely by instinct. All she could think of was Mike and how he was the only person in the world she trusted to protect her.

6

MIKE SAT IN front of his large-screen television watching *The Man Who Shot Liberty Valance.* It was past four in the morning. He'd stayed at the bar with Flip and Jack until one-thirty, playing catch-up and talking about the problems at the Speer Palace. Then he'd come back here and found he was too keyed up to sleep. He had watched *Mister Roberts* first. The oak table in front of the couch was littered with candy bar wrappers and empty packages of snacks, and now he was on his second John Ford movie of the night.

"When the legend becomes a fact, print the legend."

Mike mouthed the words along with the newspaper reporter. He knew most of this dialogue by heart but it didn't diminish his enjoyment. Every time he watched a John Ford movie, it was like a visit with an old friend.

The doorbell rang as Jimmy Stewart was making retirement noises to his wife. Mike frowned and stopped the tape. Only two people knew his private elevator code, the chief of security and Amy. It was unlikely either of them would disturb him at this hour without calling first. Mike hurried to the door and looked through the peephole. Amy was standing in the hallway wrapped in a blanket. Her face was dead white and she swayed on her feet.

"Amy! What's wrong?" Mike opened the door quickly and drew her inside. As he took her arm he noticed that her whole body was trembling.

Amy swallowed hard and tried to speak. Her mouth opened but no sound came out. Now that she was here, safe with Mike, she was weak with relief. All she could do was cling to him. Mike led her over to the couch and splashed a shot of bourbon into a glass. He knew the symptoms. Amy was in shock.

"Drink this, Amy. Don't try to talk."

Amy's hands were shaking so hard she couldn't hold the glass. Mike helped her lift it to her lips. She coughed as the strong liquor burned her throat but she swallowed obediently. Then she threw her arms around Mike's neck and sobbed.

"Hey, it's all right. Come on, Amy. Don't cry." Mike held her awkwardly. He'd dealt with hysterical women before but the fact that it was Amy who was clinging to him so desperately made Mike feel as clumsy as a teenager. The blanket slipped down around her waist and Mike gasped as he realized she was wearing nothing but a thin silk nightgown. All the desires he had suppressed surfaced with a vengeance. How delicious it would be to comfort her with a kiss that would lead to much more.

Resolutely, Mike pushed the thought back. This was Amy and she was in some sort of trouble. "All right, Amy, that's enough. Sit up and I'll get you something to wear."

It was a relief to move. Mike got up and turned his back quickly, hiding the effect Amy's nearness had created. He rushed to the closet and grabbed the first available thing, a blue velvet robe. "Put this on and I'll get you another drink, a civilized one, this time. You drink white wine, don't you?"

Amy's eyes were still glazed but she managed to nod. That was good. Mike went to the bar at the far end of the living room and busied himself opening a bottle of Chardonnay. By the time he got back, Amy had put on the robe. It covered her from head to toe and she looked much more composed than she had at first.

"All right, honey. Tell me what happened."

Mike sat down in the chair across from the couch, deliberately keeping his distance. Now she looked childishly vulnerable, and even more beautiful. Her blond hair fell past her shoulders in a tangled cloud and several strands curled tenderly against her neck. Her hands shook as she held the stemmed glass and her eyes were huge and trusting.

Amy took a sip of her wine and braced herself. Then she looked up at Mike and started to speak in a voice that trembled slightly. "Two people broke into my apartment. They tied me up, blindfolded and gagged me, drove me out to the dump south of town, and left me there. I managed to get loose and I came straight here. Their car is downstairs in my parking spot."

"Jesus!" Mike's face turned white. "Did they hurt you, Amy?"

"No. I think they were just trying to scare me." Amy took another sip of her wine. "They succeeded, Mike. I've never been so scared in my life!"

"Okay, hold on a second. I'll get Jack up here right away. Do you want me to call Flip, too?"

"No." Amy shook her head. "I'm all right now, Mike. I was afraid to go back to my apartment. I thought they might be there. You were the first person I thought of so I . . . I just came here."

"You did exactly the right thing. Just relax, Amy. I'll make a quick call and be right back."

Mike frowned as he picked up the phone in the kitchen and dialed Jack's room. He was certain Amy's abduction tied in with the other problems at the Speer Palace and he was furious. There was no way in hell he was going to let anyone hurt Amy.

Flip's hands were shaking as the taxi pulled up to Benny's Bankroll, a casino on the far end of the Marina. He'd never played here before and he was fairly sure that no one would recognize him.

"Three forty-five, mister." The taxi driver stopped by the door and took the five-dollar bill. "Change?"

"No, keep it." Flip got out of the taxi and blinked in the glare from the spotlights surrounding the entrance. Even though it was two in the morning, the flashing signs and spotlights made this area as bright as day.

Benny's Bankroll was even brighter inside. The purple carpeting flecked with gold made Flip dizzy as he hurried past the banks of slots toward the poker tables. He reminded himself that he'd just watch for a while and then go back to his room at the Speer Palace.

A chair was available at the table on the end but Flip leaned against a pseudo-Corinthian column and watched the action. Everyone said it was all a matter of willpower. Mike had no sympathy for compulsive gamblers and Flip was sure he'd lose his job if Mike ever found out.

Flip's palms started to sweat as the cards were dealt. The man in chair number one was drunk and was playing badly, and the others weren't very good either. It was a sucker's game and Flip knew he could make a bundle if he took that empty chair.

"Come on over here, buddy." The man on the end beckoned to him. "There's room for one more." Flip opened his mouth to politely refuse but his feet carried him over to the green felt table. One hand couldn't hurt. He could stop anytime he wanted.

"Good evening, sir. Would you care for a drink?" A pretty cocktail waitress rushed over.

"Uh . . . sure. Vodka straight." Flip sat down and tossed a roll of bills on the table. "Chips, please."

"All of it, sir?" The dealer hesitated.

"Yeah. All of it." Flip reached forward to rake in the piles of chips. The money he'd tossed the dealer represented his whole paycheck, but he could always cash in whatever chips he didn't use along with his winnings. It made him feel good to have more chips than the other men at the table. Flip sat back and lit a cigarette while the dealer shuffled a new deck, promising himself he'd win a few jackpots and leave. His hands were almost steady as the dealer offered him the deck and he reached out to cut it.

Jack paced the floor in Mike's suite while Mike perched on the edge of the couch next to Amy. She had told everything in a calm, rational voice but Jack had seen enough of human nature to know that she was on the edge of hysteria.

"Do you think we should call the police?"

Jack gave Mike a shocked look. "The police? In Atlantic City? I wouldn't be surprised if they were the ones who grabbed Amy."

Mike nodded grimly. It was possible. He'd given a report when the truck carrying the Speer Palace chips was robbed but the police had gotten nowhere with their investigation. There was even less to go on this time. Amy hadn't seen her kidnappers and not a word was spoken. The two men would be impossible to trace, police buy-off or no police buy-off.

"I checked on the car. It was stolen from a parking lot earlier this evening. There's no doubt in my mind, Mike. The guys were pros. There's no way Amy should stay in her apartment alone. They might come back."

Amy shuddered slightly. She knew she'd never feel comfortable in her apartment again.

"What should I do, Jack?"

Jack hesitated, searching for the right words. He'd seen the way Amy looked at Mike and he'd asked a few well-chosen questions that convinced him Mike felt the same way, although he hadn't admitted it. Mike was stubborn. Jack knew the best cure for that was to throw them together. He'd never been adverse to giving love a helping hand but he had to convince Mike that the whole thing was his idea.

"You've got two choices. I can move in with you and act as your bodyguard or you can move to another place."

"She'll have to move!"

Mike spoke so quickly both Jack and Amy turned to look at him in surprise. He looked a little embarrassed as he tried to explain his reaction.

"I'm not doubting your qualifications, Jack. I'm sure you'd keep Amy safe but I need you here at the Speer Palace, where you can keep an eye on things. I think we'd better find a new place for Amy."

Amy looked stricken. "But where? It took me a month to find that apartment."

"You can move in here, with Mike." Jack dropped the bombshell. "He's got a couple of extra bedrooms and it's a perfect setup. I can keep my eye on you during the day and at night you'll be stashed up here in a penthouse with full security and private access. That's all right with you, isn't it, Mike?"

Jack almost grinned as he saw the panicked look in Mike's eyes. It disappeared so quickly that Amy didn't notice. By the time Amy turned to look at Mike, he was nodding in agreement.

"That's perfect, Jack. I should have thought of it myself. We'll move Amy in right now. Make a list of what you need, honey, and Jack and I'll go over and get it."

"Are you sure it's all right?" Amy looked a little dubious. "I promise not to get in your way, Mike."

"You couldn't get in my way. This place is too big for that." Mike grinned at her. "Just tell us what to pack and we'll do it."

"Well . . ." Amy tried to think. "Could you bring my pillow? It's the big one on my bed with the embroidered pillowcase. And I'll need clothes. Just bring everything in the closet. You can empty the dresser by my bed and . . . Oh, no! I forgot all about Katy!"

"Katy?" Mike looked puzzled. "I didn't know you had a roommate."

"Katy's a cat. I found her raiding the garbage outside the Speer Palace snack bar and I . . . well . . . I took her home."

Mike shook his head. "No problem, Amy. There's plenty of room for a cat. Now, is there anything else I should know about? You're not operating a center for teenage runaways out of your apartment, are you?"

"No, not yet."

Mike laughed and stood up. "Come on, Jack. We'll commandeer the hotel bus and take a couple of the night men along to help us. You can watch a John Ford movie while we're gone, Amy. Snacks are in the pantry. Will you be all right here alone?"

"I'll be fine." Amy smiled at him and followed the two men to the door. She squelched the crazy urge to kiss Mike good-bye, just like a wife would kiss her husband when he went off to work. Perhaps her abduction hadn't been so awful, after all. Of course she'd been terrified while it was happening but she hadn't been hurt and Mike had asked her to move in.

The suite was huge and lonely now that Mike and Jack were gone. Amy was exhausted but she still felt too nervous to try to sleep. She found *Rio Grande*, put it in Mike's video tape machine, and went off to get a snack. John Wayne could keep her company until they got back.

The kitchen was a total surprise. Amy had expected a chrome and glass wonder with all sorts of electric gadgets but this enormous kitchen was curiously old-fashioned. The curtains were red and white checked gingham that matched the tablecloth on the slab table that took up most of one wall. There were pots and pans hanging from the exposed beams and the long wooden counter was perfect for rolling out pie crusts or kneading bread. The stove was gas, a sturdy cast-iron affair with a griddle on top. It sat on squat, fat legs at the center of the room. Amy could imagine feeding hotcakes and sausages to a whole crew of ranch hands on its ample surface. For the first time in her life, she wished she had learned how to cook.

The pantry was to the left of the stove. Amy opened the door and gasped as a light went on automatically inside. She stared at the fully stocked shelves for a moment and then she began to laugh. It was the first time she'd laughed tonight and it felt wonderful.

Mike's pantry was better than a giant refreshment counter at a movie theater. Amy picked out a package of Dots, a nickel Hershey bar that now sold for thirty cents and a bag of Planter's Peanuts. She grinned as she carried her stash back to the couch.

Amy opened all her goodies at once. There were more where they came from. It took a surprisingly short time to finish them all. Then she leaned back on the couch and yawned at John Wayne. She was asleep before he'd killed his first Indian.

It was almost dawn by the time Jack and Mike got back with Amy's things. They found her curled up on the couch sound asleep. *Rio Grande* was over. The tape player had clicked off and nothing but white noise came from the television speaker.

Mike switched off the television and motioned for Jack to follow him. They put Amy's things in the largest of the spare bedrooms and Mike made up the bed. Then he went out to get Amy.

Jack brought in the carrier with Katy and placed it by the side of the bed. The moment he opened the flaps, the calico streaked out and jumped up on the bed. heading straight for Amy's pillow where she settled down in comfort.

A moment later Mike came in, carrying Amy. Jack folded back the covers and Mike put Amy in bed. She was sleeping so soundly her eyelids didn't even flicker.

Katy took one look at Amy and backed off the pillow. She took up a position near the foot of the bed and glared at the two men. Mike and Jack exchanged glances and backed out the door, shutting it softly behind them.

"Breakfast? I can call Flip and have him join us in the coffee shop."

Jack hesitated for a long moment and then he nodded.

"That's fine with me, just as long as we don't have to eat Mandarin Burgers again."

7

DIXIE PETRELLI SAT at a choice corner table at the Hillcrest Golf and Tennis Club, waiting for her son. She had a perfect view of the manicured green lawns and impeccably trimmed trees. Occasionally a golf cart rolled by, carrying its occupants to the air-conditioned clubhouse for refreshments.

Vince's tennis lesson was over. Dixie had seen the pro come in and join the Nash sisters at their table for lunch. Rumor had it they were taking turns supporting his coke habit.

Dixie glanced at her solid-gold Cartier and decided to wait another few minutes before ordering their drinks. Vince would shower and then join her.

A smile spread across Dixie's face as she thought about her son. Vince had all the right qualities. He was handsome and athletic. He looked the part of a rich young man. Of course, he did have a few rough edges but Dixie was sure he'd grow out of them. Polish was what Vince needed and she would make sure that he got it. When Vince was born she had promised herself that he'd have every advantage that Claudio's money could buy.

Dixie's table was the best in the room and generous tipping insured that she would be seated here every time she came in for brunch. The table was near the entrance, so situated that the other members were required to pass by when they entered the room. Dixie took full advantage of that fact. She knew every member by name and net worth. She also made note of their social standing. To some members she merely nodded but others received an intimate greeting or an invitation to join her for a drink. The contacts Dixie made at the Hillcrest were worth every penny of the annual three-thousand-dollar membership fee, and if anyone happened to notice that Dixie Petrelli had never been seen to pick up a golf club or a tennis racket, it was not mentioned.

"Please bring two Ramos Gin Fizzes, Roger." Dixie nodded at the waiter who rushed up when she motioned to him. "My son should be here any moment."

Dixie's timing was perfect. The drinks arrived just as Vince came into the room. His face was flushed from recent exertion and his hair was still damp from the shower. He looked anything but happy.

"You're wasting your money on those fucking tennis lessons." Vince slid into a chair and glowered at his mother. "That asshole isn't teaching me a thing!"

"Vince, dear. Watch your language." Dixie smiled through clenched teeth and gave a little wave of her hand to the couple who had just walked in. Mr. and Mrs. Stephan Abernathy, old money. They had founded the Renaissance Art Museum. As soon as the Abernathys had moved on, Dixie's smile disappeared. "Tennis lessons are important, Vince. You know how crucial it is to associate with the right people."

Vince swallowed his angry retort and took a sip of his drink. He hated Ramos Gin Fizzes but they were very "in" with the brunch crowd this season. Vince preferred whiskey but he wasn't about to argue with Dixie this morning. He needed more money.

"Eggs Benedict, dear?" Vince nodded. His mother had been big on eggs Benedict ever since Barbara Abernathy claimed they were the best entree on the menu.

Vince decided that the time was ripe. He had a piece of news that was guaranteed to get Dixie in a good mood. His mother wanted respectability and she was willing to do anything to get it. Vince didn't care about social circles in the slightest but he let her think he did. That way the purse strings stayed open, no questions asked.

"Good news, Mom. Ronnie Abernathy asked me for mixed doubles next Saturday."

Dixie beamed at her son. The invitation for mixed doubles was a plum. Dixie didn't know that the only reason Vince had been invited was to supply the cocaine that Ronnie Abernathy needed before the match.

"I'm proud of you, Vince! The Abernathys are people worth knowing."

Vince waited until the waiter had taken their order. Then he leaned across the table and lowered his voice confidentially. "I hate to spoil our brunch with finances but I ran into a snag with our pet project. We'll need more operating capital. Say another thirty thousand?"

Dixie frowned slightly but she took out her checkbook. Money was no problem, just as long as she could guarantee that it was being well spent. "How soon will we see results, dear? I'm a little impatient."

"Very soon, Mom. The owner can't hold on for much longer. The cash is for the health inspector. He's going to find a good reason to close down the kitchen."

"Good!"

Dixie's eyes glittered as she handed Vince the check. It shouldn't be long now. There was no way a high-class hotel could operate without a kitchen. The hotel would go broke and Vince would buy it for her. As the owner of a prestigious hotel, she would certainly be accepted into the Abernathys' social circles. Claudio would have to respect Vince when he realized that his son had pulled off a financial coup all by himself. The Petrellis would be a legitimate business concern, just like the Abernathys and the Drakes, and Dixie smiled as she thought of how her life would change. No more hoodlums. No more guns. And no more corny Italian expressions about honor and family.

Vince stared at his mother. She had a dreamy sort of half smile on her face, probably thinking of all the people she'd snub when his deal came through. Vince was smart enough to play his mother's game.

"Mom?" Vince waited until he had her attention. "I've been thinking. Let's change the name, just as soon as we take over."

"The name?"

Vince grinned as his mother raised her eyebrows. The name change had come to him last night. It was inspired. It would feed Dixie's ego and get her to fork over all the cash in her checking account.

"I'd like to call the casino the Dixie Belle."

"Oh, Vince! How sweet!" Dixie dabbed at her eyes with her lace handkerchief. She reached over for Vince's hand and squeezed it affectionately. He was such a good son.

Vince smiled and squeezed back. He knew he'd made the right move. Naturally the name change would never happen. Why should he name something after his mother? She was only a pawn in his game of power. The day he bought out the Speer Palace, he would also take over the Petrelli empire. Then he could do what he'd wanted to do all his life! Tell his mother and father to fuck off.

She was running through a dark corridor and the beast pounded close behind her, gaining with every step. Amy ran as fast as her feet would carry her but there was something thick and sticky on the floor, something that made her lift her legs in slow motion, like trying to run through a puddle of rubber cement. She felt the beast's hot breath on the back of her neck and then she was tripping, falling, landing facedown. The beast was on top of her now, its fur brushing her face. It opened its mouth and . . .

"Meow!"

Katy gave a startled yowl as Amy screamed. The little calico streaked off the bed and scooted under it, peering out to glower at Amy.

Amy sat bolt upright in bed and blinked. For a moment she was totally disoriented. Then she remembered that she was in Mike's suite. She must have had a nightmare and she'd scared poor Katy half to death.

"Come on, Katy." Amy patted the bed. "It's all right. I'm awake now."

The cat inched out and hugged the far wall, staying just as far from Amy as she could possibly get. Unblinking yellow eyes stared at Amy balefully as she got out of bed and put on Mike's big bathrobe. Amy knew it would take more than a quick pat to restore their friendship but breakfast would probably do it. Katy was a sucker when it came to Little Friskies.

There were several packing cartons against the wall

and Amy found the bag of cat food in the first box she opened. She poured a generous helping into Katy's red bowl and set it down on the rug.

There was nothing like a standoff with a stubborn calico first thing in the morning. Amy tried not to laugh as Katy's tail swished back and forth. Dogs wagged their tails when they were happy but cats operated in reverse. At first Katy's tail swished back and forth like a metronome in march rhythm. Then it gradually began to slow. A waltz. A dirge. Finally it merely twitched as Katy approached her food bowl. Amy bent down to pat her and Katy purred. They were friends again.

Amy opened the bedroom door and stepped out into the hallway. The suite was silent. Either Mike was still asleep or he'd left already.

There was the aroma of hot coffee in the air. Amy followed the trail to the kitchen where a blue enamel coffeepot simmered on the stove. Amy glanced at the kitchen clock and gasped. It was almost noon. She was late for work.

There was a note propped up on the gingham-covered table. Amy smiled as she read it. *No hurry—everything okay if late or even no show—got cream for Katy—top shelf—coffee on stove—advise using cold cup.*

Amy opened the double refrigerator and laughed out loud as she saw the contents. Mike had stocked it with eight pints of heavy whipping cream. Katy would be as fat as a hippopotamus if she drank all that cream. The only other item in the refrigerator was an empty cup with *What's good about it?* printed on the side. It was obviously the cold cup in the note.

She was too groggy to figure it out but Amy took the cold cup from the shelf and filled it with coffee. After the first sip she knew exactly what Mike had meant. The coffee was steaming and the cold cup kept her from burning her lip. Leave it to Mike to think of something like that.

Two cups of coffee later Amy was ready to face the day. She poured a little cream into a saucer for Katy and went out to explore the roof garden. Half of the area was covered with grass. Amy had no idea how they'd laid in a lawn up here on the twenty-second floor but it was wonderful. Trees in huge redwood tubs were placed around the perimeter and there was a Jacuzzi in the corner. A large gas barbecue and a picnic table sat on the covered patio area.

"How about this, Katy?"

The little calico stepped gingerly onto the grass at first but in a moment she acclimated. Amy left her to chase a butterfly near one of the lemon trees and walked off to explore the area. The patio was huge and double French doors led to the master bedroom.

The room was deserted. Amy stared in at the neatly made king-size bed and sighed deeply. Then she turned and went back in through the kitchen. The master bedroom was Mike's domain. Amy knew he'd never come right out and ask her to share it but she was a lot closer than she'd ever been before.

The Jaguar roared down the incline and took a hard left, hugging the road through the nearly ninety-degree turn. Vince didn't even bother to slow for the stop sign at the bottom of the freeway off-ramp. He was late. That idiotic brunch with his mother had taken longer than he'd expected.

Vince swung into the wide blacktop lanes for the

airport and pulled up next to the restaurant bar. A valet rushed out to take the car. He looked much too eager to suit Vince.

"Forget it, kid. Nobody touches this baby but me, so leave it right here."

The attendant looked ready to protest but he turned all smiles in a hurry as Vince slipped him a five.

Cardinella's messenger was waiting for him at a table in the back. It was easy to pick him out of the crowd, even without the distinctive pin he was wearing in his lapel. He was young and nervous. And he looked totally out of place.

Vince smiled as he approached the messenger. "The job's done?"

The messenger nodded and Vince handed him an envelope. "Tell your boss there's more where this came from. I might want the same job with a different result next time. I'll be in touch."

Vince grinned as he strolled back out to his car. He'd left ten thousand dollars of Dixie's money with the messenger, five for the abduction and five for the health inspector. Another ten would be spread around to buy the loyalty he needed in his father's organization. That left ten for the buy he had coming in tonight. It was the finest shit, uncut and hot off the boat.

Moments later Vince pulled onto the expressway. Traffic was light and he reached for the vial of cocaine he kept in the glove compartment, steadying the wheel with his knees as he filled the little gold spoon. One for the right nostril and one for the left. He deserved a reward for handling that little bit of business so well.

A red Fiat pulled up in the fast lane and attempted to pass. Vince stepped on the gas and streaked forward to cut him off. The Fiat dropped back and the driver waved his fist. It was so funny Vince laughed out loud. Nothing could pass this baby when he opened her up. The huge engine purred under the hood and Vince roared past a station wagon filled with kids and a tour bus. There was a girl in a skin-tight top hitchhiking near the off-ramp and Vince cut across four lanes of traffic to get a better look.

She looked young, not more than sixteen or so, but Vince didn't stop. The young ones were more trouble than they were worth and he was in a hurry to get home. With any luck, Gina was there alone and he had one hell of a hard-on he was saving for her.

Flip wheeled his Datsun into a parking spot and got out of the car. It was so hot that waves of heat radiated from the asphalt parking lot. By the time he'd walked across the lot to the first store on Amy's list, he was dripping sweat. July in Atlantic City was impossible.

A hand-lettered sign was on the door. CURIOSITIES AND ANTIQUITIES. Flip pushed open the door and a bell tinkled somewhere in the back. The small shop was stifling inside. An antique-model floor fan made a feeble attempt to mix up the air, but it did nothing to cool the interior. An old man who had to be even older than the fan shuffled out from the rear of the store. Flip smiled, even though he didn't feel like it. It wasn't fair to take out his ill humor on an innocent shopkeeper. "I'm here to pick up a package for Miss Warner."

The man looked confused for a moment and then he nodded. "Oh, you must mean Amy. I've got it right here behind the counter. Had a little trouble wrapping it, though. Put a blanket around it first so it wouldn't poke through. Took four rolls of paper." Flip followed the man behind the counter and stared. The wrapped package was an odd shape, about three feet high and six feet wide. Flip staggered a bit as he picked it up. It weighed a ton.

"Go ahead and take it, son. Amy said she'd send over a check and I trust her. Tell her the name is Roscoe."

Flip's back was nearly breaking by the time he carried the package to the Datsun. He had to recline the passenger seat as far as it would go to get the package inside. He considered driving back to the hotel to switch the Datsun for one of the guest buses. If the rest of Amy's presents were this big, he'd be in trouble.

The next stop was an exclusive gift shop on Fifth Street. Flip sighed with relief as he walked into its air-conditioned interior. A lady in a chignon hurried up to wait on him. "I'm here to pick up a package for Miss Warner."

"Oh, you must mean Amy! It's all ready. Tell her it's one of a kind." Flip sighed as he walked out of the shop carrying the gaily wrapped package. At least this one was normal-sized. It fit neatly in the trunk of the Datsun. Now he had only one stop left to make.

The third address was in the new Midtown Mall. Flip found a parking spot right by the door and hurried up to the customer pickup desk. An older woman with carrot-red hair came to the register.

"I'm here to pick up a package for Amy," he said.

The woman frowned at him. "Amy? Is that the last name?"

Flip smiled as he spelled out the last name for her, relieved that there was at least one person in Atlantic City who didn't know his sister on a first-name basis.

8

"I'M LEAVING NOW, MINNOW."

Gina finished her lap with a burst of speed and climbed up the ladder at the deep end of the pool. Her Uncle Claudio was standing on the patio, suitcase in hand. Gina left a trail of droplets that sizzled behind her as she dashed across the sun-baked concrete to kiss him good-bye.

"Tell Vince I'll be back late tomorrow afternoon. Roberto's taking care of things while I'm gone, if he has any questions."

Gina nodded. "I'll leave a note for him, Uncle Claudio."

"A note?" Claudio frowned. "What's wrong with telling him?"

Gina thought fast. "I . . . I might not be here when he gets home."

"Regina, listen to me." Claudio looked stern. "I know you and Vince haven't always seen eye to eye but isn't it time to forget all that? Vince has changed in the last couple of months. I never thought I'd live to say it but he's growing up, showing some responsibility."

Gina nodded. She never argued with Uncle Claudio.

Claudio set down his suitcase and picked up a towel. He draped it around her shoulders and patted her awkwardly. "I'm asking a favor, Regina. Take some time and get to know Vince. Mr. Perfect he's not, but he *is* my son."

"I will, Uncle Claudio."

Gina dropped her eyes. Even though she'd been careful, Uncle Claudio had noticed how she'd been avoiding Vince. Gina wondered if she'd been too hasty. Perhaps Vince wasn't as bad as she thought he was.

A horn beeped twice and Claudio glanced toward the driveway. His car was here. "Which monkey suit did you pack for me?"

Gina smiled. "Both of them, Uncle Claudio. The blue summer weight and the brown tweed. The paper said there was a heat wave in New York right now but they expect it to end by tonight. You have your choice of six different silk handkerchiefs. I wasn't sure which color you wanted."

"Good." Claudio picked up his suitcase and gave a wave as he went through the door. Gina was a good girl. Even Dixie had to agree with him. And she'd be a stabilizing influence on Vince if the two of them hit it off together.

Paul was watching the door. When his boss appeared, he jumped out from behind the wheel to take the suitcase and open the back door of the dark-gray Lincoln. "Straight to the airport, Paul. I've got some thinking to do on the way."

Paul nodded and put the car in gear. He'd been working at his job for fifteen years now and he knew his employer's moods. Mr. Petrelli was upset. It probably had something to do with his good-for-nothing son, a description Paul often thought to himself but one he'd never voice to another living soul. He liked his job with the Petrelli organization and he wanted to keep it.

Claudio watched out the window until Paul pulled onto the expressway. Then he leaned back and closed his eyes. There was no reason why Gina and Vince couldn't make a go of it. Gina wasn't blood relation, even though she'd always called him uncle. Gina's father had been a minor man in the organization but Claudio had felt a certain responsibility when Carmen Danello was killed. He'd taken Gina into his home and he'd never been sorry. She was a good girl. She knew how to show respect and she had a head on her shoulders, unlike most Italian beauties. Vince would have to look far before he found a wife any better than Gina. Yes, Claudio decided, nothing would make him happier than to dance at their wedding.

Amy checked off the items on her list and nodded. "I'll be up there in twenty minutes to pick up the ingredients. The cake bakes for fifty minutes and then I test it, right?" Amy listened to the voice on the other end of the phone for a moment and then she laughed. Chef Sussman knew what a novice she was in the kitchen.

"No, I won't forget to turn on the oven. Thanks, Chef Sussman. You saved my life."

Amy hung up the phone and grinned. Calvin Metcalf had called an hour ago. He had needed some figures from the personnel records and they'd chatted for a few moments. Before he hung up, Calvin had asked her to give his birthday greetings to Mike.

"Today is Mike's birthday?" Amy had been surprised. Mike hadn't mentioned it to anyone.

"That's right. I'll never forget the day he was born. I

was the new kid on the staff and the accountant spent the entire day at the hospital with Nicholas. The quarterly estimated taxes were due and it was the first job Nicholas let me handle on my own."

"How did it turn out?"

Calvin had laughed. *"All right, I guess. I've been here over thirty years."*

Amy straightened her desk and locked up the office. She had a lot to accomplish before tonight. Chef Sussman had helped her plan out a simple menu, one even she could cook. Flip was out picking up the presents she had ordered and Jack was with Mike. He'd make sure that Mike stayed away from the suite until time for the party.

The elevator was crowded with smiling tourists as Amy rode up to the Dome Room. Amy smiled back. She had to pick up the ingredients for tonight's dinner, wrap the present she'd bought for Mike, decorate the patio, and bake Mike's birthday cake, all in the next four hours. She'd have to rush like crazy but it was worth it. Amy was determined to throw the best birthday party of Mike's life.

"Mr. Petrelli? My father cordially invites you to join him in the office for a drink. Will you follow me?" Claudio smiled and followed the beautiful young woman even though he knew the way. Sophia was growing up. She'd been a little girl the last time he'd been a guest in the Romanno home and now she was grown up enough to make her father worry.

"Claudio, my friend!" Giuseppe Romanno dismissed his daughter and embraced Claudio warmly. "So what do you think of my Sophia? She's changed, yes?"

"A beautiful girl, just like her mother." Claudio nodded. "She makes me feel my age, Giuseppe. I remember the day she was born."

Giuseppe sighed deeply. "Today she dances at her sister's wedding and tomorrow I start to plan her future. You're lucky you have a son, Claudio. Four daughters are a drain on a man's peace of mind."

Claudio laughed politely and handed Giuseppe an envelope. "For your daughter, Rosa. A small token on this happy occasion."

"You do me honor." Giuseppe took the envelope and placed it on his desk. Then he poured two snifters of anisette and handed one to Claudio. "I've heard rumors, Claudio. Our friendship demands that I tell you."

Claudio took a sip of his drink and met Giuseppe's eyes. The younger man was loyal. He had started out in the Petrelli organization and branched out on his own with Claudio's blessing. Giuseppe owed him a debt and Claudio knew he could trust him.

"One of my men had a conversation with Cardinella. The old man claimed he had dealings with your son, Vince. I know how you feel about Cardinella and I told my man this was impossible."

"Thank you, Giuseppe." Claudio nodded. "You have done me a favor. It will be repaid."

"It's nothing." Giuseppe picked up his glass and drained it. "Come, my friend. It's almost time for the dancing. My daughter will be heartbroken if you are not there."

Claudio walked out to the garden with Giuseppe but he barely heard the orchestra start to play. His sixty-eight years weighed heavily on his shoulders. Claudio had hoped to retire soon, but Giuseppe's news meant that he would have to keep his hands firmly on the reins of the Petrelli organization.

Alone in the house, Gina had gone out to sunbathe over an hour ago. Dixie had left for a charity auction and Vince had said he wouldn't be back before nine or ten in the evening. Relaxed and lazy, Gina had stretched out the tanning mat and anointed her body with suntan oil.

Now she was sleeping, earphones clamped tightly to her head. The tape had played all the way through three times and it was on its fourth cycle through the machine. The Woody Herman concert at Carnegie Hall, Gina's favorite jazz recording.

The sun was on its downward sweep in the sky and lengthening shadows blanketed over half of Gina's body. A warm breeze stirred her short dark hair and made dainty ripples on the surface of the pool. A dragonfly darted in a zigzag pattern over her head but Gina slept on, dreaming of something pleasant. The rosy corners of her lips lifted in a faint smile. Stan Getz's wailing saxophone in "Four Brothers" masked the noise of Vince's Jaguar as he roared up the driveway and parked in front of the house.

Vince came in through the front door and stopped to read the note Gina had left for him on the dining room table. His mother was at a charity auction and his father was gone on business. Vince smiled as he crumpled the note and tossed it toward the silver wastebasket in the corner. Things were working out just fine. Now all he had to do was find Gina.

The door to the patio was open slightly. Vince

stepped out and drew in his breath sharply at the sight that awaited him. Gina was sleeping on a mat, no more than two feet from the door. Her golden legs and arms were tinged with a rosy glow from the sun.

The sight of Gina's warm body so close to him pushed Vince over the edge. This was a perfect opportunity. He'd been playing games with Gina ever since she'd arrived this summer, staring at her, and brushing up against her whenever he could. Vince knew exactly how nervous he was making her and it was worth all the extra time he'd had to spend in his parents' house. Vince moved a step closer and pressed his hand tightly against his crotch. He knew his father would kill him if he ever found out, but he'd fix it so Gina wouldn't dare breathe a word.

Gina rolled over on her back and the top of her bathing suit slipped down slightly. The sight of her breasts drove Vince to action. He knelt down next to her on the mat and slipped her earphones off. "Hey, Gina. Wake up."

Gina opened her eyes to stare up into Vince's face. For a moment she was totally disoriented. "Vince! What . . . what are you doing here?"

Vince heard the panic in her voice and it made him feel good. He reached out and grabbed her wrists.

"I just dropped by to keep you company. I wouldn't want my little cousin to get lonely here, all by herself."

"Oh. Uh . . . I'm not lonely, Vince. Your dad should be home any minute."

Vince laughed. "Come on, Gina. I read the note. You'll have to do better than that."

Gina shuddered as she stared up at Vince, whose eyes gleamed red in the reflected light from the sun. He looked evil. Desperately, Gina played for time. "I . . . I meant your mother. I'm sure she'll be home very soon."

"We both know she'll stay at the auction until every painting's sold. We're all alone, Gina. That doesn't upset you, does it?"

"Uh . . . of course not!" Gina took a deep breath. "I'm getting cold and my suit's still wet. I think I'd better go up and change."

Vince reached up and slid the straps of Gina's suit down over her shoulders. "Here, let me help you. I don't want my little cousin to catch a cold." Before Gina could do anything but gasp in shock, Vince pulled off her suit and rolled over on top of her naked body. She tried to scream but Vince's mouth slammed against hers, bruising her lips in a passionate kiss that left her shaking with revulsion.

"Vince! Stop it, *now!*"

"I'm just helping you get warm, Gina. And in just a minute you're going to get very, very hot."

Gina struggled and kicked but Vince outweighed her by a hundred pounds and his muscles were strong from weight-lifting. Overpowering her, he forced her legs apart.

"Vince, please! Stop!" Gina's heart pounded with fear as she realized that Vince hadn't even heard her. He was intent on staring down at her body. His dark eyes were wild and he licked his lips in an obscene gesture that made her cry out in terror.

"You're going to love this, little cousin."

Gina screamed as Vince's fingers explored her roughly.

"Shut up, Gina. I didn't hurt you. I know what I'm doing." Gina's body trembled with outrage as Vince's finger probed deeply. He used his arm like a lever to pry her legs open even wider and Gina gasped as he thrust his fingers inside her, violating her most private recesses.

"You can stop pretending, Gina. I know what you want. Your pussy's hot for me."

There was a smile on Vince's face as he watched her struggle. The pupils of his eyes were pinpoints of black and Gina knew that he was high on something. She'd get nowhere trying to plead with him, appealing to the sense of morality he had never possessed. She opened her mouth and screamed for help at the top of her lungs.

"You can scream but there's no one to hear you." Vince's tone was deliberately calm, as if he were speaking to a backward child. "You might as well save yourself the trouble."

For a moment Gina was stunned. Vince was right. The nearest neighbors were more than a mile away. Desperately, Gina looked around for some way to stop him. Vince had loosened his grip on her arm and Gina managed to pull it free. Then she reached up and clawed at his back with all her strength. Her nails raked deeply into his skin, drawing blood, but Vince only laughed.

"Go ahead, Gina. I like a little fight in my women." Suddenly Vince was kneeling over her, knees on either side of her shoulders. He grabbed her arms, wrenching them up over her head with one hand as he pulled his pants down with the other.

"I've been saving this just for you, little cousin." Vince freed his huge erection and smiled down at her. "Now be a good girl and show me what you can do with that nice hot mouth of yours."

For a moment the meaning didn't register. She stared up at him in total shock as he bent closer, aiming the tip of his swelling shaft at her lips.

"Vince! No!" She tried to turn her head away but Vince was holding it too tightly. There was a ringing in Gina's ears and she felt faint. He couldn't force her to do this. She'd rather die.

Gina reacted automatically. She clenched her teeth together and shut her eyes, shivering uncontrollably. She wanted to scream for him to stop but she didn't dare open her mouth.

"Cut the crap, Gina. I don't want to get rough with you . . . unless I have to."

Vince's voice was still soft but Gina heard the undercurrent of menace. Her eyes flew open in surprise as his hand clamped down over her nose.

"All right, Gina. You can't say I didn't ask you nice. We both know you have to come up for air sometime and it won't kill you to lick it a little."

Gina held her breath until her head was whirling and she knew she was about to pass out. At last her body won out over her will. Her lips parted in a desperate gasp for air and Vince lunged forward. Gina gave a strangled cry. Retching, she felt as if she were suffocating, choking on the sheer size of him, on the shame of this moment. Tears sprang to Gina's eyes and rolled down her cheeks.

After a long moment, Vince gave a snort of disgust and pulled back. "Next time I'm gonna teach you a few things about cocksucking. Right now I got more important things on my mind." Vince reached for her breasts and twisted the nipples between his fingers so hard that Gina screamed again. Then he grabbed her legs, forcing them apart with his powerful hands.

"Vince . . . No!"

There was panic in Gina's voice but Vince didn't seem to care. He held her immobile and battered the head of his thick shaft against her until she gave way to the sheer force of his attack.

"Jesus! That's tight!" Vince gave a groan of pleasure as he rammed in all the way. "Come on, Gina. Give me a good fuck!" Gina struggled but she couldn't twist away from him. She was pinned down, caught like a butterfly in a display case as he hurtled forward.

It was a nightmare. Gina shut her eyes and prayed for it to end but Vince slammed her down against the mat again and again. She managed to get hold of his neck with her teeth and she bit down savagely but Vince merely swatted her off as if she were a troublesome fly.

There was no way of telling how much time had passed. The tinny strains of "Blues in the Night" floated up from the headphones by the side of the mat and Gina knew she'd never be able to listen to that song again. Vince's body was slick with sweat and the warm salty drops from his body dripped down on Gina's face and stung her eyes. At last it was over. Vince's heavy body shuddered and was still. Then he got to his feet. "You better shut up about this. I get mean when I'm crossed."

Gina lay motionless, staring up at the sky above her and trying to escape into the recesses of her own mind. She'd never known what hatred was until now.

Vince reached down with one hand and yanked Gina to her feet. His fingers found her throat and squeezed tightly. "You hear me?"

Gina nodded. There were spots in front of her eyes and her knees sagged weakly when Vince released her at last. There was no doubt in her mind that he'd kill her if she told anyone what had happened.

Vince turned his back on her deliberately and pulled on his pants. Then he walked to the open patio doors and turned around to face her again. "I gotta find the time to teach you some tricks, little cousin. You're a lousy lay."

9

JACK HUMPHRIES SAT at the huge conference table in Mike's office. He closed the last folder and added it to the pile of papers he had finished reading. They chronicled the problems at the Speer Palace, from the delayed building permits before the foundation was excavated to the discovery of the slot machine cheater two nights ago. He could see why Mike was worried. Everything fit.

Mike had told him about his meeting with Claudio Petrelli. Jack had heard stories about the don and he'd formed his own conclusions. Claudio was shrewd and ruthless, a tough customer all the way. Lots of people held grudges against the Petrelli organization but Jack had never heard any of them claim that Claudio Petrelli was a liar.

Jack made a mental note to call in some markers in the morning. He had several minor hoodlums who owed him favors, and one of them was bound to have heard something. When he looked up he found Mike staring at him.

"Well? Do you think there's something here or am I just being paranoid?"

"Nope." Jack looked grim. "You've got yourself a

powerful enemy, Mike. We have to find out who. And why."

"It's almost a relief to hear you say that." Mike drew a deep breath. "When things first started happening, I thought it was just a run of bad luck. I still remember what my father went through when he started the Barcelona Palace. Everything went wrong. After the first year, the board wanted him to sell and cut his losses but he held on. Now it's the biggest money-maker in the chain."

"How long do you have to bring this one around?"

"A little more than a month."

Jack whistled. "You didn't cut yourself much slack, did you?"

"It's internal board politics, Jack. There was a take-over plan against my father but Cal and I bought enough stock to gain a controlling interest. When I was nominated for president, the board was divided. It was a deadlock between the original board members who felt they owed something to Nicholas, and the new blood. You know the type. Pinstripe suits, alligators on their underwear, and M.B.A.s from a private school that Daddy supports."

Jack nodded. "The bottom-line boys. They don't give a damn about quality, just profits."

Mike reached for the carafe of coffee and poured himself another cup. He took a sip and sighed deeply. "Well, I won. Six to five, one abstention. That was when I proposed the plans for this place. The board wouldn't give me more than a minimum budget and a year to show a profit. The way things stand right now, we'll be bankrupt long before that."

"Could the whole company go broke?"

Mike shook his head. "Not a chance. Speer International's doing fine but I'll be out in the cold. I've been selling off my stock to meet expenses. I figure I can hang on another four weeks, maybe six at the outside. Then I fold my tent and steal away in the night . . . unless my secret weapon works."

"What's your secret weapon?"

"You."

Jack laughed but it sounded false to his own ears. There might be no problem in finding out who was behind the attack but stopping them was another matter. Mike needed more than a good detective if he was up against the big boys.

Just then the intercom buzzed and Mike reached out to answer it.

"Mr. Pierce again? All right, Judy. Tell him to hold for a minute."

Jack looked up as Mike motioned to him. "R. D. Pierce is on the line. He represents a block of investors who made an offer on the Speer Palace last month. I turned them down flat. Pierce is probably going to make me another offer."

"Good." Jack smiled. "Tell him Jack Humphries, your business manager, will drop by to see him within the hour. Then we'll see what we can learn about Mr. Pierce."

"Six-thirty? Yes, I can make it. The name? Uh . . . hold on a second, please."

Gina reached for the telephone book and flipped it open. She picked a name at random. "Jensen. That's J . . . E . . . N . . . S . . . E . . . N. Right. Mary Jensen."

Gina hung up the phone and raced to the closet. Now that the shock had worn off, all she wanted to do was run.

She had stayed on the patio until Vince's Jaguar had roared out of the driveway. Then she had forced herself to move, to take her robe and wrap it around her chilled body. She had sat huddled on a patio chair for a full five minutes until she was sure that he had truly left.

A nearly scalding shower had eased some of the stiffness in her body but nothing could erase the memory. She didn't dare tell Uncle Claudio. She had to run away. But where? Suddenly Gina had remembered the card she'd gotten over two months ago with the color picture on the front. Amy had a new job in Atlantic City.

Gina grabbed clothes at random and stuffed them into her suitcase. She snapped the bag shut and glanced at the clock by the bed. She had plenty of time to catch her flight and once she made it to Atlantic City, she'd be safe. Now Gina was glad she'd kept her home life a secret from everyone. Amy didn't know that she lived with Claudio Petrelli and Uncle Claudio had no idea who Amy Warner was. There would be no way for Uncle Claudio to trace her and Gina had no intention of telling Amy that she was the runaway niece of an important Mafia don.

Gravel crunched in the driveway as a car pulled up. Gina's heart pounded hard in her chest. Vince?

A horn sounded twice and Gina breathed a sigh of relief. It was her taxi. Gina raced down the stairs, the suitcase bumping awkwardly against her legs. She ran out to the waiting cab, not even bothering to lock the house behind her. "The airport. And hurry!"

Gina held her breath as the taxi navigated the long, winding driveway. She didn't relax until they turned onto the expressway and headed toward the airport. Vince would never be able to catch her now.

"Which airline, lady?"

Gina stopped herself just in time. Vince might have her traced. She said the name of the first airline that popped into her mind. "Pan Am. I'm catching the seven o'clock flight to Los Angeles."

The driver swung into the airport and pulled up at the Pan Am terminal. "You want me to carry your bag inside for you?"

"No, thank you. It's fairly light."

Gina handed the driver a ten and told him to keep the change, a fifteen percent tip. If she overtipped or undertipped, he might remember her.

A redcap rushed up to take her bag but Gina waved him away. She lugged it inside the terminal and watched out the glass doors until the taxi pulled away. The shuttle bus was right on schedule. Gina arrived at the Mercury Airline ticketing desk a full forty-five minutes before her flight, the length of time the airline had recommended.

There were only four people in line and Gina got behind a harassed-looking mother with a toddler on one arm and a baby in the other. The toddler was pulling on his mother's hand, asking for some toy that was packed in a carry-on bag. A young couple was second in line. They wore washed-out jeans with college sweatshirts and Gina noticed that they were holding hands. They looked young and very much in love.

Gina studied the man at the head of the line, a businessman type with a full set of matched luggage. Every few moments he glanced at his watch and looked disgruntled. After observing the reservations clerk for a moment, Gina understood.

The ticket agent seemed to be having trouble with the computer. She punched in code after code and glared at the terminal. After at least ten minutes of punching in numbers, she made a call for assistance and went to sit on a stool near the window, totally ignoring the people in line.

"Miss?" The man at the counter looked impatient. "If that computer's not working, couldn't you move us all to another window?"

"I'm sorry, sir. I'm only authorized to work at this station."

"Could you write out our tickets by hand then?"

"I'm sorry, sir. All tickets must be validated by the computer."

The man shrugged and gave up. Five minutes passed before an officious-looking airline executive strolled up to the counter. He wore a red jacket with an insignia on the lapel.

The clerk explained the problem in whispers and the airline's official fiddled with the keyboard for a few minutes. Then he shook his head and both of them walked away, leaving the counter entirely unmanned.

It was another five minutes before they came back, accompanied by an older woman with glasses on a chain around her neck. She flipped a switch on the computer, punched in a code, slipped on her glasses to read the display and gave the printer a sharp whack with the side of her hand. Everyone breathed a sigh of relief as it activated and the ticket rolled out.

"Next, please?"

The businessman with his matched set of luggage moved up. The clerk frowned as she looked at his bags.

"I'm sorry, sir. All luggage must be tagged with Mercury labels."

"But my bags have tags. They're right here on the handles."

"I'm sorry, sir. It's for your own protection. All luggage must be clearly marked with Mercury Airline tags."

The man started to fill out the tags, grumbling a bit. Then he realized that he was holding up the line.

"You can wait on someone else while I'm doing this. It'll take a couple of minutes."

"I'm sorry, sir, but Mercury's promise of personal service requires that we deal with only one customer at a time."

Gina shifted from foot to foot. If things didn't speed up soon, she'd miss her plane.

At last the man at the counter had his luggage tagged to the clerk's satisfaction. Gina moved up one place in line and glanced at the clock. The flight would leave in less than fifteen minutes. Unless it was delayed for some reason, she'd never make it.

The young couple had everything prepared in advance but the clerk insisted on verifying their identification before she would give them their prepaid tickets. They needed a major credit card and a valid driver's license for identification.

"But I don't drive!" The girl looked upset. "I can give you two major credit cards. Is that all right?"

"I'll have to check with the office. Just a moment, please." The clerk left the window and went to another station to use the phone. By now there were close to twenty people in line and some of them were beginning to voice their dissatisfaction. If Gina had seen something like this in a television comedy, she never would have believed it. Another few minutes passed before the clerk came back and told the girl that they had decided to make an exception in her case.

The young mother moved up to the counter and Gina sighed when the clerk asked for verification of the children's ages.

"I have their birth certificates right here." The young mother smiled. "I've flown Mercury before."

Finally it was Gina's turn.

"I have a reservation on flight two-seventeen. The name is Jensen. Mary Jensen."

The clerk punched some numbers into her computer and shook her head as she read the screen.

"Oh, I'm sorry. We'll have to reschedule that. Flight two-seventeen has already boarded. Didn't the telephone helper tell you to be here forty-five minutes early for processing?"

It was the final straw. Gina glared at the inept clerk and slammed her purse down on the counter. "I *was* here forty-five minutes early! I spent the entire time waiting in this line. Now, I want you to pick up your phone and tell that flight to wait."

"I'm very sorry, but I don't have the authorization to do that."

"Then get it! It's taken you a total of forty-four minutes to ticket four passengers. You really don't want me to talk to your supervisor, do you?"

The clerk shot Gina a startled look and reached for the phone. Gina heard her tell someone to hold the plane.

"Will that be cash or charge, Miss Jensen?"

"Cash. I don't have to show you two pieces of identification for that, do I?"

Someone in the back of the line snickered and the

clerk had the grace to blush. "No, Miss Jensen. Cash is perfectly acceptable."

Gina winced as she handed over the money but she knew she didn't dare use her credit card. After paying for the ticket, she was left with less than forty dollars. If Amy wasn't home, she'd be in big trouble.

"Thank you, Miss Jensen. You have seat forty-two C. That's on the aisle. The plane is waiting for you at Gate Twelve."

Gina grabbed her ticket and rushed for the gate. She heard a noise behind her and turned. The other passengers in line were applauding.

10

AMY SAT IN a chair by the kitchen table, sipping a cup of coffee and watching the birthday cake bake through the glass door of the oven. Chef Sussman had just left after delivering the cake batter. He'd guaranteed that it was the richest chocolate cake in existence. Just as soon as the cake had baked and cooled, Amy would frost it with Chocolate Wonder icing, a sinful confection made with chocolate, powdered sugar, and cream cheese. Amy knew it would have been simpler if Chef Sussman had prepared the cake in the Dome Room kitchen but this way she could truthfully claim she'd baked it herself.

The aroma coming from the oven made Amy's mouth water. It reminded her that she hadn't eaten all day. There hadn't been time.

Amy knew she didn't have Mike's talent for thinking up novel ways to dress up burgers, so she'd raided Chef Sussman's pantry, picking out the things that might strike Mike's fancy. In addition to the traditional toppings, she'd selected dates, coconut, golden raisins, and a jar of maraschino cherries. If Mike had the inclination, he could make himself a tutti-frutti burger.

Katy came in through the open patio door and brushed up against Amy's leg. When she was sure she had Amy's attention, she sauntered over to the refrigerator and sat back on her haunches to stare soulfully at the closed door. Katy was no fool. She had already finished one bowl of cream and she had figured out that the mother lode was inside.

"No more cream today, Katy." Amy shook her head. "There's food in your bowl if you're hungry."

Katy ambled over to her bowl and sniffed disdainfully. After a long, hard look at Amy, she picked up one piece of dry cat food in her teeth and trotted back out on the patio. Amy sighed as the little calico buried it in her litter box. It hadn't taken long to change Katy's eating habits.

The timer on the stove rang and Amy got up to test the cake. Since none of the batter stuck to the thin wooden skewer Chef Sussman had given her, she took it out of the oven and put it on a rack to cool. It would be at least an hour before she could frost it. Perhaps she should stretch out on her bed and take a nap. She hadn't gotten much sleep last night.

Jack and Mike had brought her alarm clock and Amy plugged it in, setting it to wake her in an hour. Then she curled up with her special pillow and tried to think relaxing thoughts.

She pictured a peaceful stream, meandering through a forest. Wildflowers lined its banks and the sun filtered through the trees on the shore, casting ever-shifting patterns on the water. A graceful doe with her spotted fawn came down to the brook. A mother bear, leading her cubs. A raccoon, the masked bandit of the woods. A family of otters who washed their food in the stream. They were followed by the smaller animals. Bushy-tailed squirrels, chipmunks, field mice, and . . .

Rats. Amy's eyes popped open. There had been rats at the dump last night, huge brown rats with eyes that gleamed red. She didn't dare think about that or she'd never get to sleep. She remembered an anecdote one of her English professors had told in college. A famous author, member of an exclusive gentlemen's club, became irate when he found all the tables in the dining room occupied. He suggested a criteria for limiting membership. All newcomers would be required to stand in a corner for five minutes and not think about a white bear.

It was impossible. Amy reached out to shut off the alarm. There was only one way to forget about last night. She had to keep busy. First she'd hang up the clothes Mike and Jack had brought from her apartment and then she'd choose something to wear to the party tonight.

The closet in Mike's guest bedroom was huge. Amy's clothes filled only a third of the space. She took out a white rough-knit Perry Ellis dress and eyed it critically. Wearing white at a barbecue was inviting disaster. She'd be sure to spill something on it.

Amy gave a deep sigh as she assessed her wardrobe. The outfits she wore to work were too businesslike. This was a festive occasion. Rita had given her a black silk Kamali jumpsuit for Christmas last year but it was much too formal for tonight. She needed a hostess outfit, something that would give Mike the impression that she was comfortable entertaining his friends.

Suddenly Amy remembered the flowered sundress she'd seen in the boutique downstairs. She still had at least thirty minutes before the cake would be cool and that was just enough time to run down and buy it.

Amy giggled as she grabbed her purse and raced out to the elevator. The flowered sundress was something that Valerie Jeffries wouldn't be caught dead in, but

Amy had decided to be herself, and damn the consequences. Valerie Jeffries might be more sophisticated, but she hadn't managed to move in with Mike!

Jack gave a low whistle as Mike stopped at a red light. The woman crossing the street was wearing white shorts and her legs were long and shapely. She had to be a dancer.

"Keep your mind on business, Jack. You've got a job to do." Mike grinned at his friend to take the reproach out of his words.

"Right." Jack leaned back in the seat. "How do you stand it, Mike? You're surrounded by gorgeous dancers and cocktail waitresses."

Mike nodded. "It's a matter of discipline. I make it a policy never to date the employees."

"I assume that policy doesn't include the guests. I was with you when you got that call from Mrs. Jeffries this morning."

"Well . . ." Mike swung the Porsche around a corner. "There's an exception to every rule."

"Some exception! I saw her at the front desk."

Mike laughed as he drove into the Pierce Towers parking lot and paid the attendant. "So what do I do now? Sit in the car and wait for you like a chauffeur?"

"No. You make yourself useful by going to that bank across the street and keeping your appointment with the president. His name's Lowell Chapman and he went to Yale, class of fifty-eight." Jack reached into his pocket and handed Mike a pin. "Wear this in your lapel. You were there fifteen years later but they were still talking about Lethal Lowell's end run in the game against Harvard. Tell him you have an offer on the Speer Palace and you're checking to see that Mr. Pierce has enough capital to stand behind his offer. If you play on the old boy network, he might spill something important."

Mike turned to look at Jack in surprise. "When did you have time to find out all that?"

"While you were having my business cards printed. I sure hope the ink is dry. Oh yeah, be sure to ask for cognac when he pours you a drink. He's got a private stock of World War II stuff that'll knock your socks off."

Jack waited until Mike had crossed the street, then pushed open the double glass doors of Atlantic City's newest high-rise office building. Mr. Pierce was obviously an affluent businessman. The lobby was air-conditioned and Jack took a deep breath of the cool air. He straightened his tie and walked toward the elevator. He always felt uncomfortable wearing a suit but Mr. Pierce wouldn't take him seriously unless he looked the part.

Jack felt his stomach drop down to his ankles as he was whisked skyward. A bell rang, the doors opened, and he found himself standing in front of a mahogany door polished to a high gleam. A small brass plaque was set in the center of the door. R. D. Pierce & Associates had the whole twelfth floor. Jack pushed open the door and found himself in a waiting area, decorated with mauve carpet and light-gray walls. Mauve and gray prints of flowers hung in silver frames at eye level and there was a grouping of gray leather chairs against the walls.

"Good afternoon, sir." A receptionist, wearing a gray silk dress with a mauve scarf, appeared almost immediately. "Do you have an appointment?"

"Yes. Jack Humphries to see Mr. Pierce."

The receptionist glanced down at his card. "If you'll have a seat for just a moment, Mr. Humphries, someone will be right with you."

Jack sat on a chair near the door and watched the receptionist disappear into the recesses of the office, wondering if all Mr. Pierce's employees were dressed in gray and mauve. He could hear the faint clatter of typewriters somewhere in the distance and the muted ring of a telephone. The door to the inner offices opened again and another woman came out, also dressed in gray silk with a mauve scarf. It must be boring as hell working on the twelfth floor.

"Mr. Humphries?" The second woman gave him a professional smile. "I'm Miss Murphy, Mr. Pierce's confidential secretary. If you'll follow me please?"

Jack followed the woman down the corridor. Noticing that she had lovely red hair pulled back tightly into a bun, he was almost surprised her job description didn't require that she dye it to match the decor. They passed several closed mahogany doors. One door was open and Jack peeked in. More gray and mauve flower prints. They must have gotten a deal.

The secretary paused at the mahogany door at the end and knocked softly. Then she opened it and ushered Jack in. "Mr. Humphries to see you, Mr. Pierce."

R. D. Pierce was predictably gray, from head to toe. He was a small man in his fifties, dwarfed by a huge mahogany desk. Gray hair, stylishly cut. Gray suit with a dress shirt of a lighter shade. Dark-gray tie. Jack found himself wondering whether Mr. Pierce wore mauve underwear. "Please sit down, Mr. Humphries. Colleen? Pour coffee for Mr. Humphries."

Jack watched as the woman poured coffee into a

china cup and handed it to him. As he let his fingers touch hers, the secretary blushed slightly.

"That will be all, Colleen."

Jack gave her a wink as she turned on her heel and headed for the door. The color rose in her cheeks and she glanced at her boss apprehensively, but he hadn't noticed.

"I spoke with Mr. Speer and he confirms that you are his authorized representative. As you know, R. D. Pierce and Associates has tendered an offer to buy the Speer Palace."

Jack nodded. "A ridiculously low offer. Mr. Speer was . . . amused. He sent me over to find out why you bothered him."

Mr. Pierce was not rattled in the least. "R. D. Pierce and Associates has learned that the Speer Palace is operating in the red. Naturally the offer reflects this downward trend. Our group of investors isn't in the habit of bidding on successful businesses, Mr. Humphries."

"Piranhas, right, Mr. Pierce? They attack only the wounded."

Mr. Pierce permitted a slight smile to pass over his face. "You might say that. The business world doesn't run on charity, Mr. Humphries. Our investors are concerned with buying as low as possible, turning the business around, and selling at a considerable profit."

"Just who is this group of investors? Mr. Speer always likes to know who he's dealing with."

"R. D. Pierce and Associates has been authorized to handle all negotiations. I personally received verification of the new offer on Tuesday. The identity of the investors is confidential . . . and entirely immaterial, I might add."

"Until you can tell me who your investors are, we're not interested." Jack put the bone china cup firmly in its saucer and stood up. "Mr. Speer likes to call his enemies by name."

As he opened the door Jack glanced back and noted happily that Mr. Pierce looked a bit flustered. Jack couldn't resist. "You really ought to wear a different color suit," he commented. "That shade of gray makes you look like a corpse."

Colleen Murphy was coming down the hall in time for Jack's parting shot, and he saw that she was having trouble keeping a straight face.

"How do you stand it?" Jack took her arm. "There's something wrong with a man who decorates his office to look like a gloomy day." Colleen tried to look shocked but her lips turned up at the corners.

"And why doesn't he dress you in emerald green to match your smiling Irish eyes?"

"Oh, Mr. Humphries!" This time Colleen laughed, and Jack waltzed her down the hallway and into an office with her name on the door where he collapsed in a chair and mopped his forehead. "Could I ask you to get me a glass of water? I think that waltz did me in."

Colleen giggled. "Right away, Mr. Humphries. "Wait here and I'll bring you some."

The moment Colleen left, Jack hurried to her desk. She was an efficient secretary and her Rolodex was on top. Jack checked the cards under *P*. Palomar Corporation, Paker & Associates, Paso Robles Inc., Petrelli . . . The area code on the card was Chicago and Jack nodded. It was all beginning to fall into place. He was back in his chair when Colleen came back.

"You're a lifesaver, Colleen." Jack gulped the water and stood up. "I'd invite you to go dancing but I have to fly out to Chicago tonight. I just hope Western's got a flight."

"If they don't, try Midwest." Colleen gave him a smile. "They have flights every hour. Mr. Pierce took a Midwest flight to Chicago last Tuesday."

Jack smiled as he rang for the elevator. Thanks to Colleen, he knew that Pierce had flown to Chicago. And Petrelli's name was in his secretary's Rolodex. Mike might not think the Mafia was behind the attempt on the Speer Palace but Jack was stacking up some pretty powerful evidence.

Mike propped his feet up on his desk and leaned back in his chair. He'd sampled Mr. Chapman's excellent cognac and learned that R. D. Pierce had deposited a large retainer from Chicago on Wednesday. Jack had just nodded when Mike had told him but he'd said it was too soon to make any assumptions.

It had been a long day. Mike yawned and glanced at his Rolex. Six-ten. July fifteenth. Today was his birthday and he'd forgotten all about it. Mike swallowed hard as he remembered his childhood birthdays. When he was a kid, his father used to throw parties at fabulous places and invite two of Mike's friends to come along. It was something Mike had looked forward to all year.

When he was six, they'd gone to Disneyland, unlimited riding all day and dinner in the private executive dining room overlooking the park. Another year they had gone to the San Diego Zoo for an entire weekend. The year that Mike had started reading *The Adventures of Tom Sawyer,* Nicholas had rented a riverboat and they'd traveled down the Mississippi.

As Mike grew older, the birthday celebrations had

spread to other continents. Mike had received a set of leather-bound Sherlock Holmes books from Calvin one Christmas. Mike had been fascinated by the super sleuth. That year, on his birthday, Nicholas had taken them to 222B Baker Street, where an official from Scotland Yard had retraced the famous detective's footsteps through London.

The succeeding years were just as special. There had been the rodeo weekend in Argentina, the fishing trip in Alaska, visits to all the exciting places that most kids only saw in movies or read about in books. Nicholas had made a point of tailoring every birthday to Mike's current interests and he'd never been wrong.

Mike laughed out loud as he remembered his fourteenth birthday party. He'd been so careful to keep his *Playboy* magazines hidden from Nicholas but none of Mike's interests escaped his father's attention. That year there had been just the four of them, Nicholas, Mike, Flip, and Jack. They'd flown to Hugh Hefner's Playboy Mansion for a huge birthday party with all Mike's favorite centerfolds in attendance. The bunnies had been charming and the boys had been awestruck. They had gone back to Thorton that fall with piles of autographed photos that were worth their weight in gold and Mike had a special memory of one little bunny named Mitzi.

His eyes were wet and Mike blinked hard. This birthday, the first one without his father, would have been terribly depressing without Amy's barbecue. Of course, she had no idea that it was his birthday but she'd called him earlier this afternoon and asked if it was all right to invite Jack and Flip for dinner on his patio at seven.

Mike had been amazed at Amy's ability to bounce

back after her scare last night. Most of the women he knew would have taken to their beds for a week. Instead, Amy was throwing a barbecue. He'd promised to be upstairs by seven and there were two stops he had to make first.

Mike felt good as he got into the elevator and rode down to the florists. It was damned nice of Amy to go to all this work and the least he could do was take her some flowers.

"Good evening, Mr. Speer. We just got in a shipment of lovely yellow roses." Mike's favorite florist, Fred Smithers, was working tonight. The bespectacled little man knew all there was to know about flowers and his unusual arrangements were the envy of every other floral shop in town.

"Not this time, Fred. I need something different." Mike wandered over to the display case and looked inside its refrigerated interior. A single yellow rose was Mike's trademark, a thank-you after an enjoyable evening in bed. Not at all right for Amy.

"How about an arrangement of blue and purple columbines? There's an old story that if you grasp the leaves, you gain courage."

"This lady already has courage. What are those pink flowers on the left?"

"Gillyflowers. They're quite delicate. Some people believe you can use their leaves for divination."

"And the little white ones?"

"Lilly of the valley. They supposedly sprang up when a saint was wounded while fighting dragons. We also have some beautiful tiger lilies, Mr. Speer. They're the orange flowers in the middle of the case."

"Tiger lilies?" Mike began to grin. "They're perfect, Fred. These flowers are for Miss Warner."

"Oh, for Amy!" Fred brightened. "Do you want them sent to her office, Mr. Speer?"

"No, I'll take them myself. Make up a nice arrangement, Fred, and I'll pick them up in a couple of minutes. I have to stop at the wine shop first."

Mike came out of the wine shop carrying three bottles of the Zaca Mesa Zinfandel that the clerk had recommended. Fred had the arrangement of tiger lilies ready and moments later Mike was in the elevator, riding up to his suite. He glanced at his watch and grinned as he realized he was as excited as a teenager on his first big date.

Amy licked a dab of chocolate off her finger and began frosting the cake. Flip and Jack were out on the patio, working on the Happy Birthday banner. Katy crouched behind a bush in attack position, the tip of her tail flicking slightly. Amy knew what that meant. There would be cat prints on the banner before long.

Frosting a cake was harder than it looked. Amy had watched Chef Sussman accomplish the job with a few deft strokes but she couldn't seem to spread the frosting evenly. The crumbs stuck to her knife and it was taking forever. Finally Amy finished to her satisfaction and stepped back proudly. Now all she had to do was put on the decoration.

"What do you think, Amy?"

Flip and Jack stood at the open patio door, holding the banner between them. It was hand-lettered in two different styles and there were cat prints between the words but Amy thought it looked just fine.

"Perfect." Amy nodded gravely. "It's a work of art. Can you two manage to hang it alone? I still have to write the message on this cake."

"Sure." Flip reached out to dip his finger in the frosting and Amy slapped his hand. He made a face and looked wounded.

"Oh, here." Amy laughed. "Take this bowl with you. There's plenty of frosting left to scrape out."

Amy got out the tube of cake gel and cut off the tip with a paring knife. Chef Sussman had told her he didn't approve of using commercial products but there was no way he could teach her to master a pastry tube in one day. He said the gel would work just fine as long as she didn't attempt to do more than write HAPPY BIRTHDAY on the top of the cake.

Amy planned out the letters in her head. Happy Birthday was so bland. She wanted Mike to know that this cake was homemade. Perhaps she could squeeze in a few more words and personalize the message.

She was about to start writing when Flip called out from the patio.

"The sign's up. You'd better hurry, Amy. He'll be here any minute."

Amy squeezed the gel out of the tube and wrote the letters as quickly as she could. She had decided on *Have a Happy Birthday, Mike.* Everything went perfectly until she got to the final *E* in *MIKE.* She had miscounted the letters and there was barely room to sneak in a very skinny *E* that hugged the very edge of the cake. Amy sighed as she stepped back to examine her work. At least it was personalized.

The doorbell rang just as she finished. Amy put a cover on the cake and rushed out to answer it. Jack and Flip were in position, standing under the banner next to the pile of presents. Amy smoothed back her hair, adjusted the strap on her sundress, and opened the door.

"Hi, pretty girl! I like that dress."

Amy grinned as Mike bent down to kiss her on the cheek. She'd been right about creating her own style.

"These are for you." Mike handed her a bouquet of flowers.

For a moment Amy was flabbergasted. It was the first time Mike had ever given her flowers. "Oh, thank you, Mike!" Amy threw her arms around his neck and kissed him. They were beautiful, and it was a start. She knew she could work her way up to a single yellow rose one of these nights. "Come out on the patio. Flip and Jack are here already."

The moment Mike stepped through the doors, Jack and Flip started singing. Amy laughed and joined in. Mike didn't seem to mind that they were all off-tune. When they were finished he applauded.

"I never expected anything like this. How did you know it was my birthday?"

Flip grinned. "Amy told us. We remembered that it was sometime in July but we didn't know the exact date."

"Calvin Metcalf said it was today." Amy led Mike over to the couch. "He called me for some figures and told me to wish you a happy birthday."

Just as soon as Mike was seated, Jack went to the bar to mix him a drink. Flip handed him the smallest package.

"Amy arranged for the presents. You've got to work your way up, the smallest to the biggest. I'm dying to know what's in that big one. I almost broke my back getting it up here."

Mike tore off the wrapping and uncovered a video tape of *The Tornado,* John Ford's first silent film.

"How did you ever find this?"

"Ask Amy."

Amy blushed a little as Mike looked at her. "I called the New York Museum of Modern Art and they gave me a list of private collectors. I located a man in New Jersey who had a print, he duped it for me, and I had it transferred to video tape at a shop in the Midtown Mall."

"Good work, Amy." Jack nodded approvingly. "You'd make a fine detective."

Mike teased Katy with the tip of the ribbon from the first present. The little calico made several attempts to catch the end as he pulled it along the floor.

"Come on, Mike." Flip handed him another present. "You'll never get to the big one this way."

Mike didn't waste any time. He tore off the paper and tossed it on the floor so Katy could bat it around. Everyone leaned closer as he lifted the lid off the box.

"A doll?" Jack looked puzzled but Mike started to laugh.

"It's a John Wayne doll! Look at this. It winds up."

Mike set the doll down on the coffee table and wound the key on its back. John Wayne swaggered forward five steps and drew his guns. Then he swiveled around, firing in all directions.

Jack laughed. "Where did you find it, Amy?"

"I met a woman who makes dolls to order while I was looking for new products for our gift shop. Open the big one, Mike. Flip's dying of curiosity."

Mike bent down to lift the package onto his lap and changed his mind. Flip was right. It weighed a ton. He knelt down beside it and tore off the wrapping. There was something inside, wrapped in a blanket. Katy approached the blanket and sniffed as Mike loosened it.

Then she let out a startled yowl and backed off hissing, her hackles raised.

"It's a moosehead!" Mike grinned from ear to ear. "Relax, Katy. This animal's dead and stuffed."

Mike picked up Katy and petted her. Then he turned to Amy. "How did you find out that I've always wanted a moosehead?"

"I didn't." Amy shrugged. "It just seemed appropriate, somehow. His name's Roscoe. The man at the antique store told Flip."

"What a great birthday! This really means a lot to me."

Mike swallowed hard and got up to hug Amy. He felt good, better than he had in a long time, and it was all because of her. Jack's suggestion last night had been a regular brainstorm. He was really beginning to enjoy sharing this place with Amy.

11

GINA STEPPED INTO an empty phone booth and pulled the door shut to block out the garbled messages from the loudspeakers. Now she knew why people never answered their pages at airports. They couldn't understand them. Her fingers were shaking as she dialed Amy's number for the fifth time in the past hour.

She let the phone ring twenty times before she gave up. It was past eleven and she'd hoped Amy would be home by now. The thought of drinking another cup of what passed for coffee in the airport restaurant made Gina's stomach twist up in knots. She knew she should have taken the time to call Amy from Uncle Claudio's house but she hadn't wanted a record of her call. And now Amy wasn't home.

Gina reread the postcard Amy had sent her: *Working at Atlantic City's newest casino. Great job. Lousy hours. Up to fourteen a day but it's worth it. Explain when I see you. Come for a visit? Telephone listed in book.*

A man in a gray suit tapped on the glass impatiently. He looked desperate to use the phone. Gina stuck the card back in her purse and vacated the booth. She'd been so upset when she couldn't reach Amy's home number, she hadn't even thought of contacting her at the casino. Amy was probably still at work. She hadn't mentioned the name of the casino but it shouldn't be that difficult to find out.

The girl at the Hertz booth was flipping through a magazine, looking bored. She stashed it quickly under the counter when Gina walked up.

"May I help you, ma'am?"

The girl smiled and Gina smiled back. It was the friendliest smile Gina had seen tonight. Hertz had hired the right person for this spot. "This is going to sound crazy but do you know the name of the newest casino in town?"

The girl looked flustered. "Oh, gosh! I'm really sorry but I don't. I just moved here from Miami and I haven't even been on the Boardwalk yet."

Gina thanked her and started to go but the girl called her back. "Ma'am? Let me make a couple of calls. I bet I can find out for you."

"That's really nice of you but are you sure you have time?"

"Time's all I've got tonight. I haven't had a customer in two hours. Let's check with the telephone company first. Maybe they've got a separate list of new numbers."

Gina perched on a stool at the counter while the girl dialed. The operator she reached didn't have that information but she connected them with her supervisor. The supervisor gave them the number of the local chamber of commerce and they ended up with a recorded message saying that the office would open at nine in the morning.

A tall man with two suitcases came rushing up to the

counter. Gina climbed off her stool and offered it to him.

"Go ahead, sir. I'm not renting a car."

"No, please don't get up. I've been sitting on the plane for three hours. Right now it's a relief to be able to stand."

"May I help you, sir?" The girl behind the counter flashed her perfect smile.

"I hope so. The name's Morgan. I called in for a reservation."

"I have it all ready for you, Mr. Morgan. A Cadillac Seville, with power steering and air. Is that right?"

"Right."

"You're all set, Mr. Morgan. Someone will bring the car right up to that door over there. Would you like one of our complimentary maps?"

"No need. I've been coming here every summer for ten years. I'm staying at the hottest casino on the strip this time, the Speer Palace. It's new."

"Oh, thank you, sir!"

Both Gina and the Hertz girl spoke in unison and the man looked startled. These Hertz employees certainly were friendly.

Amy lit the candles in the kitchen and carried the cake out to the patio. She was proud of her effort. It looked very professional.

"Chocolate?" Mike asked as she set it down on the table in front of him.

"What else? I baked it myself. Make a wish and blow out the candles."

Mike shut his eyes and wished that the troubles at the Speer Palace would be over, then blew them out. "It's a wonderful cake, Amy. Look guys, it says . . ."

Mike looked down at the cake and started to laugh. He turned it so Flip and Jack could see the message and they all cracked up.

Amy rushed over. "I don't see what's so funny," she said, a bit huffily. "The *E* doesn't look *that* bad."

"Oh, Amy!" Mike reached out to draw her close. "Read it out loud, word by word."

"It's perfectly clear. It says, 'Have a Happy . . .'" Amy stopped and stared. "Oh, no! I forgot to put in *Birthday.* It says, 'Have a Happy Mike.'"

"Well, you *do* have a happy Mike. Bring your plate over, Amy. You get the first slice."

Vince pulled into the garage and swore as the Jaguar's headlights illuminated his mother's Mercedes. That threw a royal crimp in his plans. Gina had whetted his appetite this afternoon and he'd driven back to his parents' house for a quickie. He took the small gold vial from his glove compartment and sampled the coke he'd just bought. It was every bit as good as his contact had promised. Another round with Gina was out but, now that his mother was here he'd hit her up for some cash. He had plenty of time to make it back to his apartment for the party.

Dixie was sitting on the couch in the living room, sipping a dry martini. She looked up as he came in. "Hello, dear. Where's Gina?"

Vince shrugged. "I don't know. Isn't she here?"

"I don't think so. The house was dark when I came home and I assumed you two were together."

"I haven't seen her, Mom, but I'll go up and check her room."

Vince's palms started to sweat as he rushed up to

Gina's room and opened the closet. Her suitcase was gone. The dumb little Guinea had run away.

"Aw, shit!" Vince picked up the extension phone by Gina's bed. He had to cover his ass fast.

"Ray? This is Vince. Call in a couple of men and have them meet me at my apartment right away. We got a big problem."

Dixie looked up as Vince came down the stairs. "Did you find her, dear?"

"No, Mom, but I invited her to a party at my apartment tonight. She must have left early to have her hair done or something."

Dixie smiled. "I'm glad you invited her. The poor girl hasn't been out of this house since she arrived."

"That reminds me, Mom. Could you spare a little cash? I want to make sure Gina has a good time."

Dixie sighed but there was an amused smile on her face. "You're always running short, dear. My purse is on the hall table. Take what you need and we'll settle up later. Will you be driving Gina home? I don't want her riding with someone we don't trust."

"Sure, Mom, unless she wants to stay over in my extra bedroom."

"Talk her into it, dear. You shouldn't drive when you've been drinking and I won't worry as long as Gina's with you."

Vince stopped at the hall table on his way out and removed five hundred dollars from his mother's purse. Then he drove to his apartment as fast as he dared. He'd bought himself a little time with his mother, but the old man was due home tomorrow afternoon. There'd be hell to pay if Ray's boys hadn't found Gina by then.

* * *

"So you can see that it's really important that I contact her. I don't know another soul in Atlantic City."

Gina finished explaining her situation again, this time to the chief of security at the Speer Palace. She'd already talked to the clerk at the reservations desk and the bell captain.

"I think I can reach her by phone. Hold on just a minute, Miss . . . ?"

"Gina. Just tell her it's Gina. She'll know who I am."

The chief picked up the phone and dialed a number. "Hank, here. I've got someone who wants to see Miss Warner. She says her name is Gina and she's from out-of-state. . . . Five-three, dark hair, slight build. Right. I'll put her on." The chief nodded and handed the phone to Gina.

"Gina? I thought you were in Chicago!"

Gina was so glad to hear Amy's voice she almost cried. "I was but . . . well . . . I'll tell you all about it when I see you. Where are you?"

"I'm right here in the hotel. Stay with Hank and I'll be right down."

Gina handed the phone back to the chief. "She said I should stay here, she'd be right down."

The chief nodded. He looked much friendlier now. He had no sooner poured Gina a cup of coffee than Amy came through the door, took one look at Gina, and rushed over to hug her.

"It's all right, Hank. Mike sent his thanks for being so cautious. Come on, Gina. Grab your suitcase and let's go. I've got a big piece of chocolate cake waiting for you."

Gina waited until they had left the office and even then she lowered her voice. "Are they always so careful with their employees? I was afraid they wouldn't even let me talk to you."

"There's a reason. . . . Two men tried to kidnap me last night."

"My God!"

"Don't look so worried, Gina. I wasn't hurt. It's a long story and I'll tell you all about it when we've got time."

Gina winced as they walked into the casino. The sound was deafening at first, with slot machines ringing and silver clinking in the trays. Amy led her past the blackjack tables and Gina's eyes widened as she spotted a sign designating a hundred-dollar minimum bet. There were six people playing at the table.

"All those people must have money to throw away."

Amy glanced at Gina and burst out laughing. "You've got the right idea, Gina. The odds are always in the house's favor."

The back of the casino was quieter. Gina walked past the baccarat alcove, with its deep-red velvet drapes. The people at the tables looked wealthy and the atmosphere was hushed and refined. Gina could tell that the stakes were high.

"Are the odds still in the house's favor here?"

Amy nodded.

"Then why do they gamble?"

"Each person thinks he'll be the lucky one to beat the odds. Occasionally someone does. And that's just enough to keep the others trying." Amy stopped in front of a bank of elevators and pushed a button. The doors opened and Gina followed her inside. The moment the doors shut behind them, all the noise disappeared. "Better?"

Gina nodded. "I guess I'm just not used to it."

"You'd be surprised how little time it takes. After a couple of minutes on the floor, I don't even notice it."

Amy punched in a code and the elevator rose. "Okay, tell me what you're doing in Atlantic City."

Gina hesitated. Now she was glad that she'd never mentioned her uncle by name. Some instinct had stopped her, even though Amy had been her best friend at Fairview. Gina had simply explained that she was living with relatives after the death of her parents and Amy hadn't been the type of friend to pry into Gina's past.

"I had some free time, so I decided to pay you a visit. I know I should have called first, but I . . . I left in a hurry. Man trouble. I . . . I don't really want to talk about it yet."

"Bad break for him, lucky break for me." Amy laughed. "I'm really glad to see you, Gina. How long can you stay?"

"Well . . . I was actually thinking about moving here, if I can find a job. Do you suppose you could let me bunk in with you for a week or so, just until I get my first paycheck?"

Amy started to laugh. "Gina, you're a godsend! I've got about ten jobs to fill and no applicants. You can take your pick."

Gina gave Amy's arm a little squeeze as they left the elevator. "I'm so glad I found you! All I need right now is that chocolate cake."

"Gina!" Flip rushed up to greet her as they came in. "You're all grown up."

"I hope so." Gina laughed and hugged him. "You haven't seen me since I was twelve."

"Jack Humphries is here, too."

"Oh, good." Gina grinned. She remembered Jack

very well, as a big kid with red hair and freckles whom she'd had a terrible crush on that summer.

"Jack's helping Mike hang his new moosehead. You remember Mike Speer, don't you? He's the kid who climbed after all those Frisbees you girls lost on the roof."

"Mike Speer? Of course." Gina shook her head. "You know, I didn't even connect. He owns this place, doesn't he?"

Flip nodded. "Come out on the patio. They've been waiting for you."

"Hi, Gina." Jack turned with a warm smile. He was about twice as big as Gina remembered and a lot more handsome.

"It's good to see you, Jack."

The man on the top of the ladder finished hanging the moosehead and turned to climb down. Gina gasped when she saw his face, recalling his visit with Uncle Claudio.

"Gina!" Mike came over to hug her. "It's been a long time."

"Not so long as all that." Gina gave him a shaky smile.

12

HELEN BURKHOLTZ STEPPED out of the shower and wrapped herself in one of the Speer Palace's fluffy bath towels. She shook off the drops of water that clung to her shower cap and hung it over the showerhead to dry. A glance in the mirror assured her that her hairdo was still intact. Roger had given her a hundred dollars at dinner and told her to have a good time while he attended his evening meetings. She'd spent thirty on a new blouse at the boutique and forty-five in the hotel beauty shop. That left twenty-five for mad money.

It was after eleven by the time Helen finished dressing. She was wearing her new blouse and a favorite wraparound skirt. She examined her reflection in the mirror and smiled. The girl at the beauty shop had been right—she did look years younger with a liquid base makeup and blue eyeliner. Helen picked up her purse and switched out the lights as she left the room. She knew she didn't have to be concerned about the electricity here but old habits were hard to break. Roger'd had to remind her not to make the bed again this morning.

She walked to the elevator, swinging her hips the way she had when she was a teenager. Roger was meeting her at the entrance to the showroom at ten minutes to twelve. They had tickets for the midnight show. It was their last night in Atlantic City, the National Optometrists' Convention was over at noon tomorrow, and both of them had decided to stay up and enjoy the casino. They could sleep on the plane when they flew back to Cedar Rapids tomorrow afternoon.

A bellhop came down the hall and Helen smiled at him. He smiled back. "Good evening, Mrs. Burkholtz."

Helen's smile grew wider. Imagine a bellhop remembering her name! The staff was so friendly here she almost hated to go home.

"Thank *you,* sweetheart. Be sure to ask for me the next time you come to Atlantic City." Donna Jacobs stuffed the bills in her shoulder bag and gave her best professional smile. This one had been easy. An optometrist from North Dakota. He hadn't wanted anything fancy, just a straight half hour, no frills. She had one more trick to turn and she could go home for the night.

She turned at the door and looked back. The john was sitting on the edge of the bed, looking depressed. He'd confessed that his wife wasn't interested in sex anymore. Now that the kids were grown, she'd even moved to a separate bedroom. Donna supposed she shouldn't feel sorry for him. If all the wives in this country acted as nice as the hookers, there wouldn't be any business left for her.

"Hey. Cheer up, Tiger. I haven't had this much fun in a long time and that's a compliment. I'm certainly in a position to make comparisons."

That got a wide blink of amazement, then a big smile. Donna walked back to the bed and stood looking down at him. He was a nice man. Maybe she could help him out a little. "Do you have an extra handkerchief, Tiger? I've got an idea."

The john took a handkerchief out of his suit pocket and handed it to her. Donna blotted her lips and made sure she left a nice ring of red lipstick.

"Just leave this in your suit pocket. When your wife asks, tell her someone at the convention borrowed it. Don't say another word, even if she pushes you. I bet she'll move back in your bedroom within a week."

The man laughed out loud and Donna went out into the hallway smiling. Leave 'em laughing. It was good for return business, not that she'd be in this business for much longer. Two more months of classes and she'd be a certified dental hygienist. It would be a switch to put things in other people's mouths.

Donna sighed as she pressed the button for the elevator. She had almost an hour before she was due in Room 682, more than enough time for a cup of coffee and a sandwich. Tomorrow was her day off. She never worked on Sundays. She usually slept until eleven, did her laundry in the afternoon while she studied, and attended evening services at the Presbyterian church. The other girls who worked the Speer Palace thought that Donna's religious scruples kept her from booking tricks on Sunday. The rumor gave her a certain amount of class. If the truth were known, Donna didn't think that working on Sunday was sacrilegious, it was simply impractical. Everyone knew that Sundays were the slowest day of the week.

"Could you zip this for me, honey?" Carole Schuman stood with her back to her husband, Mel, her new red dress half on. She leaned back against him as he zipped it up.

Mel took his time. Carole had a very sexy back. He turned her around and kissed her on the lips. "Are you sure you want to go to that show? I can think of some interesting things we could do right here."

"We've been right here for the past six hours." Carole laughed and kissed him back. "At least give the maid a chance to make up the bed."

"You'd better take that package out from under your pillow first."

"What package?" Carole rushed to the bed and drew out a silver wrapped box. "Oh, Mel! I thought we agreed that this weekend was our anniversary present."

"Just a little something I picked up this afternoon."

Carole smiled as she tore off the wrapping. If they'd been at home, she would have unwrapped it carefully to save the ribbon and paper for another round. She felt wildly extravagant as she tossed the wrapping on the unmade bed.

"A diamond pendant?" Carole gasped as she lifted the lid. "Oh, honey. We can't afford something like this!"

"Sure we can. I won a little extra at the crap table while you were swimming. I think it'll look perfect with that slinky new dress."

Carole beamed as Mel hung the chain around her neck. The little heart-shaped diamond pendant glittered in the light and she felt like a princess. Now she was glad they'd decided to splurge on their first anniversary.

It had seemed like the height of extravagance to stay at a hotel in Atlantic City when they could drive there and back in less than an hour. They lived only twenty miles away, in an apartment complex by the manufacturing plant where they both worked.

Mel had insisted. They'd been saving up for a house and they'd barely gone to the movies since they'd been married. A weekend in Atlantic City would be good for both of them. Carole had given in with one stipulation—only if Mel could find a good deal.

Mel had paged through the ads in the Sunday paper, and at exactly noon today, the earliest time for check-in, Carole and Mel had arrived at the Speer Palace to use their two-fer: two nights for the price of one, with a free bottle of champagne and a midnight show.

"Come on, honey. The show starts in ten minutes." Mel gave his wife a little squeeze and led her toward the door. "I called room service. Our bottle of champagne'll be waiting for us when we get back."

Carole smiled as they walked down the hall. Sometimes Mel had fantastic ideas. She'd never dreamed that staying at the Speer Palace for a weekend could be so exciting.

Gina opened her suitcase and took out slacks and a sweater. Flip, Jack, and Amy were taking her on a guided tour of the casino while Mike supervised the count at the cage. She still felt a little strange at barging in on Amy like this but Mike had insisted she stay in one of the extra bedrooms in his suite. There was a knock at the door and Amy walked in. "Almost ready? Flip begged off but Jack and I want to take you to the Dome Room. The view's fantastic. Mike should be through working in about an hour and we'll all meet back here."

"Is this outfit all right? I . . . I packed in a hurry and I didn't think to bring something fancy."

"You look just fine. Anything goes in Atlantic City. You'll see men in tuxedos and women in formal gowns but most people wear whatever's comfortable."

"Amy?" Gina reached out to take Amy's hand. "Are you sure it's all right for me to stay here? I . . . I don't want to interrupt you and Mike."

Amy sighed and shook her head. "There's nothing to interrupt, Gina. Mike still hasn't made a move in my direction. Nothing's changed since we were at Fairview."

"No other men in your life?"

"There was one, but it didn't work out."

"It's still Mike then?"

Amy nodded. "Don't say it—I know it's crazy. I lived with a man in New York for almost a year. My friends said he was perfect for me but every time we made love, I imagined he was Mike."

Gina winced. "You've got a real problem, Amy. But at least you're living with him."

"But I'm not sharing his bed. That's why he insisted you stay here, Gina: Mike doesn't want to be alone with me."

"I see . . ." Gina looked thoughtful for a moment and then she started to smile.

"Oh, oh. I recognize that smile. What are you thinking, Gina?"

"Nothing much," Gina shrugged. "Why don't you stay here, Amy, and wait for Mike to come back? Jack and I have so much to talk about that I wouldn't be a bit surprised if we stayed out all night."

Flip walked down the green carpeted hallway and caught sight of his reflection in one of the gilt-edged mirrors decorating the walls. There were bags under his eyes and his hands were shaking. Last night's poker game had cost him his sleep as well as his paycheck.

He turned the key in his lock. A good night's sleep would do wonders for his depression. He felt so damn helpless. If he'd had a little more money, he might have turned the odds around . . . but Flip had promised himself he wouldn't fall into that trap again. He'd had his fling and from now on he'd stay away from the tables.

Flip took off his clothes and let them drop to the floor, too tired to hang them up, then crawled into bed. After a few restless moments, Flip knew it was hopeless. As he stared up into the darkness a bitter expression crossed his face. He'd do better adding up the markers he'd signed in Nevada and Jersey than counting sheep. They were covered, but the price he'd paid was too high.

Gina and Jack were in a booth at the Dome Room, watching the waitress open their wine.

"Some people call this a 'blush,'" their waitress explained. "This particular bottle is a Blanc de Noir. That means 'white of black' in French. We also have a Sauvignon Blanc and a Pinot Noir Blanc. The wineries in California started bottling these wines about five years ago and they've become very popular. The skins from the grapes are removed at a strategic point in the fermenting process, which makes the color lighter and the taste more delicate than you'd expect in a red wine. At the same time, blushes have a much fuller body and a richer bouquet than the whites."

Jack looked impressed. "You seem to know a lot about wines."

The waitress smiled and poured a sample of the

bottle for Jack. After he nodded, she filled their glasses. "Before I started working here, the only thing I'd ever tasted was my grandmother's dandelion wine. Mr. Speer says it's impossible for us to recommend a good wine unless we're familiar with it. Every time we add a new label to the menu, he tells us about it and we have a tasting."

Gina tried the wine and smiled. "Well, you certainly recommended the right wine for me. This is just perfect."

"How about a small cheese plate to go with it? Chef Sussman has a very good Brie tonight."

"That sounds good." Jack looked amused. "Do you get to taste the cheese, too?"

"We taste a little of everything, sir. I've gained five pounds since I started working here."

As soon as the waitress had left, Jack pointed to the view of the city. "Look around you, Gina. We're on an island, surrounded by water. The Indians called it 'Absecon.' That means 'place of swans.'"

"Atlantic City's beautiful at night." Gina sighed. "I had the strangest feeling when I rode over here in the taxi. I know I've never been here before but everything was so familiar. Park Place, New York Avenue, Boardwalk . . ."

Jack laughed. "Go directly to jail. Do not pass Go. Do not collect two hundred dollars."

"Monopoly?" Gina looked stunned. "You're right, Jack! It used to be my favorite game."

"The board's based on Atlantic City. Look down at the grid the streetlights make, Gina." She moved closer to the glass and looked out but she kept one hand tightly on the edge of the booth. Heights always made her feel faint.

"The original streets were laid out in 1824. The ones that run in from the beach have state names and the cross streets were named for the seven seas."

"Atlantic, Pacific, Mediterranean, Baltic . . ." Gina stopped suddenly. "I was always lousy at geography, Jack."

"Caspian, Adriatic, and Arctic. I'm lousy at geography, too, but I read about it in a brochure I picked up at Mike's travel shop. There was a movement in 1973 to change the names of Baltic and Mediterranean but there was such a public outcry from the nation's Monopoly fans that the city council voted down the proposal."

Gina laughed. "You're a wealth of information, Jack. You can sit right here and tell me the history of Atlantic City. And if you get tired, we can always ask our waitress to explain the whole wine list. I figure between the two of you, you can keep me amused for the next six hours."

"Six hours?"

Gina sighed. "I'm afraid so. I told Amy I'd probably stay out all night. I wanted to give her a chance to be alone with Mike."

Jack looked amused. "Are you trying to play matchmaker?"

"No, I'm just playing absent. I tried matchmaker when Amy and I were roommates at Fairview. Amy and I tried every tactic in the book on Mike but nothing happened."

"You had a crush on Mike, too?"

Gina felt her face grow hot. "No. Actually, I had a crush on . . . on you!"

"You did?" Jack looked delighted. "I wish you'd said

something. I wonder if it was the same year that I got interested in you."

Jack reached out and touched the rim of his glass to hers. "A toast to old loves. And to new."

Gina laughed as she raised the glass to her lips, feeling wonderfully comfortable and safe. An hour passed and they managed to demolish the cheese platter and drink their way through the bottle of blush. Jack drained the last of his glass and smiled. "Let's go down and browse in the shops. I promised Mike I'd keep my eye on a couple of new people he hired."

"That sounds like fun." Gina got to her feet a bit unsteadily. She'd had much more to drink than usual.

"I've got to stop at my room, first. You can see my view of the pool."

"No!"

Jack turned to look at her in surprise and Gina realized she'd spoken much too loudly. This was Jack, not Vince. She had nothing to be afraid of.

"What's wrong, Gina?"

"It's a long story, Jack. Maybe I'll tell you someday." Gina tried to smile but she could tell it came out wrong from the worried expression on Jack's face. "I . . . I just overreacted, that's all. Of course we can stop by your room."

"Are you sure?" Jack still looked concerned.

"Positive." Gina took Jack's arm as they waited for the elevator. By then her panic had begun to subside and she managed to give him a genuine smile as the elevator arrived.

13

HELEN BURKHOLTZ SMILED at the happy-looking young couple who got on at the sixth floor. The man was tall with short brown hair and Helen noticed that he was having trouble keeping his glasses from sliding down his nose. If Roger were in the elevator right now, he'd probably talk him into a pair of extended-wear soft lenses.

The woman was wearing a low-cut red dress with a pair of gold sandals that were so obviously new she hadn't quite learned how to walk in them yet. She smiled as the doors slid closed and reached up to touch the heart-shaped pendant that nestled at the base of her throat. The side walls were mirrored and the young woman patted her hair. "It's a good thing we don't have elevators like this where I work," she said, turning to Helen with a smile. "All the secretaries would be putting on makeup between floors."

Helen nodded. "I do volunteer work at a preschool in Cedar Rapids. Can you imagine what a group of four-year-olds could do to these mirrors? We'd go broke buying Windex."

"Cedar Rapids?" The young man looked interested. "I have a cousin there, Doug Jacobson. He's in the remodeling business."

"He did my kitchen last year! I guess it really is a small world."

They were in the midst of exchanging names when the elevator stopped on the fifth floor and a pretty young woman got in. Her makeup was flawless and her dark hair was cut stylishly. Helen guessed she'd had it cut in the beauty shop downstairs. All three of them smiled at her and she smiled back.

"Are you going to the show, Helen?" Carole, the girl in the red dress, resumed their conversation. "We heard it was fantastic."

"My husband, Roger, is meeting me there. Maybe we could all share a table."

"Try to sit near the center if you can." The dark-haired woman spoke up. "There's a wonderful number where the showgirls wear shoes that light up. I saw it last weekend with a . . . with my boyfriend, John."

The bell rang and the elevator stopped at the third floor. The doors opened and two men got on. The taller one wore a tweed jacket with patches at the elbows and a pair of polyester slacks. His eyes were slightly bloodshot and Helen knew Roger would prescribe an eyedrop for cosmetic reasons but that wouldn't solve the man's problem. She could tell by looking at the broken veins in his nose and his flushed skin that he was a chronic drinker. The smaller man was approximately Roger's height, about two inches shy of six feet tall. His sandy hair was a little shaggy over the ears and he looked uncomfortable in his brown, ill-fitting suit. He was carrying an old-fashioned briefcase, the kind Fuller Brush salesmen used to use, and his hands were shaking slightly.

Helen smiled at the men but they avoided her eyes,

staring impassively at the doors until they closed. Then the taller man pushed the stop button with one hand and reached into the breast pocket of his jacket with the other. At first Helen couldn't believe her eyes. It was the same kind of handgun she'd seen on *Columbo* reruns, and the barrel was pointing straight at her!

His voice was gruff in the sudden silence. "Do what you're told and nobody gets hurt. Wallets, purses, and jewelry. Pass 'em over." He waved his gun slightly and Helen bit back a scream. "You first, lady!"

Helen gulped as she realized the man was talking to her but somehow she managed to hand over her evening bag. The sandy-haired man opened his briefcase and dropped it inside. Thank God she'd left her grandmother's antique ring back home in Cedar Rapids!

Carole cringed as the tall man aimed at her. All the color had left her face and she trembled as she dropped her purse into the open briefcase. "Please don't take my pendant!" Her voice was high, like a terrified child's. "It's my anniversary present."

"Just give it to him, honey." Mel dropped his wallet into the briefcase. "He's got a gun."

The gunman laughed as Carole unclasped her necklace. It was a chilling sound. "Smart man you've got there, lady. Now drop it in."

The dark-haired woman didn't say a word as she handed over her purse and earrings. As soon as his briefcase was closed, the gunman put the elevator in motion again. The whole robbery had taken no more than a minute. "Now listen to me real careful." There was menace in the tall man's voice. "We're gonna get off at the next floor but you're going all the way to the top. Smile nice and stay inside if you want to keep healthy."

When the doors opened the man with the briefcase looked out, nodded, and they backed out of the elevator. Helen leaned against the mirrored wall and drew a deep, shuddering breath of relief as the doors slid closed and the car rose straight up to the Dome Room.

"Is something wrong?" Jack followed Gina into the elevator and hit the stop button. The passengers inside looked shell-shocked.

Mel opened his mouth but nothing came out. He cleared his throat and tried again. "We were robbed! Two men. One had a gun."

Helen nodded. She'd recovered some of her composure. "They got on at the third floor. I guess we'd better report it."

"I'll take care of it, ma'am." Jack flashed his Speer Palace security badge.

"I feel like a coward." Mel looked embarrassed. "Maybe I should have tried to hit the emergency bell or something."

Jack shook his head. "You did exactly the right thing. It's never wise to cross a man holding a gun. Now I want you all to come down to the office with me. Mr. Speer will want a list of the items you lost so he can reimburse you."

"I'm supposed to meet my husband for the midnight show." Helen's voice shook a little. "He'll be worried if I'm not there."

"No problem, ma'am. I'll send a runner to get him. There's another show in an hour and I'll make sure you have the best seats in the house."

Jack turned. "I'll need your help, Gina. Will you go to the house phone and call Mike? Ask him to meet us in his office."

Gina nodded and got out of the elevator. She'd never seen anyone take charge so quickly. How strange that Jack should remind her of her Uncle Claudio.

Amy tested the water in the Jacuzzi with the tip of her toe and drew it back quickly. She'd probably end up looking like a lobster.

Mike was in the living room, opening another bottle of Dom Pérignon. Amy knew she'd had more than enough champagne already, but a little more couldn't hurt. She gave a mischievous grin as she dropped her towel and stood in the darkness. The warm breeze caressed her bare skin; she hadn't bothered with a bathing suit. Amy giggled and tossed her towel over Roscoe's head. That was better. She'd better hurry and get into the water before Mike came out the door. Amy stifled a squeal as she climbed into the Jacuzzi. It was scalding at first but, after a moment, it felt marvelous. She leaned back against the tiles and let the water swirl around her body. Pure heaven.

Mike appeared in the doorway, holding two glasses of champagne. He laughed as he spotted the towel-draped moosehead. "Why'd you spoil Roscoe's fun?"

"He was staring at me."

"I see. Maybe I didn't need to open that last bottle of champagne, after all. It sounds as if you've had plenty."

Amy giggled and wondered whether Mike's white bathing trunks would turn transparent in the water.

"Here's to you, Amy." Mike raised his glass. "That was a wonderful birthday party."

"I'm so glad you liked it." Amy stifled another giggle, amused at how prim and proper she sounded. But proper matrons never sat in their Jacuzzis naked, at least she didn't think they did. Suddenly Amy wondered if she'd gone too far. Mike's fingers brushed against hers as he handed her the glass and she shivered slightly, feeling like a fool, now grateful for the darkness.

Mike slid into the water next to her and stretched out. A scant inch of water separated their bodies. Amy had all she could do not to jump up and dash for her room. Whatever had possessed her?

"Look at those stars. There's nothing like relaxing in a hot tub after a long day."

Mike draped a friendly arm around Amy's waist. It was nice sharing his Jacuzzi with Amy. It got lonely up here all by himself. He took a sip of champagne and set his glass down. Amy was one of his favorite people. Her skin was so soft and so . . .

Bare. Amy's skin was bare. Mike moved his fingers up slightly, expecting to feel a bikini strap any second. Her back was one gorgeous expanse of soft, silky, warm, bare skin. Mike's self-control snapped and he pulled her to him abruptly.

Her hair smelled of violets and Mike groaned as he kissed her. Her breasts pushed up against his chest and his fingers found them, caressing the soft heated curves with a will of their own. Christ, but she was beautiful, more beautiful than any other woman he'd had. How could he have waited so long?

Dimly Mike heard the phone ring. His lips were on Amy's as he lifted her out of the water and set her on the edge of the tub. Her lush body glistened with drops of water that looked like diamonds in the moonlight.

He buried his face in the valley between her breasts, nuzzling, kissing . . .

The phone rang again. Mike shook his head to clear it. Something was wrong. His staff had orders never to use this number unless it was an emergency. "Damn!" Mike got to his feet and threw Amy a towel. "I've got to answer that, Amy."

Amy shivered. She could hear Mike in the kitchen and he sounded upset.

Instead of crying, she wrapped the towel tightly around her body and headed for her room. If she'd known the damn phone was going to ring, she would have ripped it right off the wall.

It took Mike less than five minutes to dress and get down to the floor. On his way he stopped the first cocktail waitress he saw and had her follow him. The five people in his reception room looked up as he came in.

"This is Mike Speer." Jack introduced him to the robbery victims, one by one. "These people are making out lists of the items they've lost."

"Good." Mike nodded. "First, let me apologize for what happened tonight. Naturally, the Speer Palace will replace your valuables and I'd like to talk to each of you in just a moment. Order anything you'd like while you're waiting and Mary, our waitress, will bring it to you."

Mike motioned for Jack and they went into his inner office. "Well, Jack, what do you think? Is this another setup?"

"Probably," Jack nodded. "These are all nice people, Mike, and I don't think they'll cause any trouble but they're pretty shaken up."

"Of course they are!" Mike swiveled around in his chair and stared out at the pool. "Okay, Jack. You've done a great job calming them down so far. Give me a minute and then show the Schumans in."

The robbery victims were understandably upset and Mike knew it would be harder to set them at ease if he sat behind his huge wooden desk. He walked to the gas fireplace on the far wall and switched it on. The air-conditioning was kept at a constant sixty-eight degrees and the fire made his large office feel cozier. Then he dimmed the lights and arranged four white leather chairs in a conversational grouping around a low mahogany coffee table. He had just finished setting out a carafe of coffee and ashtrays when Jack knocked on his door and ushered in Carole and Mel.

"Come and sit over here by the fire." Mike greeted them and led them to the comfortable leather chairs. "I'm really sorry this happened and I'd like to make it up to you if I can." Five minutes later the Schumans were smiling happily at the news that the Speer Palace was picking up the tab for their entire weekend.

"Now, let's see that list of yours." Mike took the list Mel handed him and scanned it quickly. One item, a heart-shaped diamond pendant, had been purchased in the hotel jewelry store this afternoon. At least that would be easy to replace. He looked up and smiled at the young couple. "The store is open all night, Mel. Just give them this charge slip."

Mel Schuman looked nervous as he reached out for the slip. "Thank you, Mr. Speer. We really appreciate all this, especially the free room and the dinners and all."

"It's the least I can do." Mike stood up and shook the younger man's hand. Mel Schuman was a nice guy.

He'd said he was carrying only twenty dollars in his wallet and most guys would have claimed much more, under the circumstances.

"Uh . . . wait outside for me, will you, Carole. I have to talk to Mr. Speer for a second."

Carole Schuman shook Mike's hand also and left the room. Mel waited until the door was closed before he started talking. "That pendant wasn't really a diamond, Mr. Speer. It was only zircon. I gave it to Carole for our anniversary tonight and it was all I could afford."

Mike nodded. "Thanks for telling me, Mel. You pick out a real diamond this time."

Mel swallowed hard and then he grinned. "Thanks, Mr. Speer. I'm sure glad we came here for our anniversary."

Jack showed Donna Jacobs in next. She smiled at Mike and perched on the edge of a chair. "Don't go to any trouble for me, Mr. Speer. I heard what you did for Mel and Carole but my earrings were just dime-store stuff. I did have fifty dollars in my purse, though."

"I know you did, Donna. From Room 563, right?"

Donna blushed and nodded. "Can I go now, Mr. Speer. I've got a . . . a date in ten minutes."

"Sure, Donna, but take this with you. I figure we owe you for at least an hour of your time. A hundred, right?"

"Right." Donna nodded. "But you don't have to do that, Mr. Speer. I was between rooms at the time."

"Stop at the boutique and pick out a new purse. It's on the house."

"Hey, you're all right, Mr. Speer. If you ever feel like . . . well . . . my number's in the book."

Mike chuckled as Donna left. He still wasn't entirely comfortable with the call-girl setup, but every big hotel had them. At least the girls who worked out of the Palace were well protected and they didn't have to cut in the bell captain. Donna was a bright girl and Mike was glad that her work here was temporary. He'd see what he could do about placing her with a good dentist when she graduated.

As soon as Donna had left, Jack ushered in Helen and Roger Burkholtz. The only item Helen had listed was the twenty-five dollars she'd carried in her purse.

"Twenty-five dollars?" Mike smiled at her. "Surely you had more than money in your purse. Most women I know carry handbags that can double as suitcases."

Helen laughed. "You're right, Mr. Speer, but tonight I was carrying my evening bag and there's not much room inside. All I had with me was a lace handkerchief, the money and . . . and some pictures of my grandchildren."

Mike noticed the hesitation in Helen's voice when she mentioned the pictures. "How long has it been since you've seen your grandchildren, Helen?"

"It's been over a year. My daughter lives out on the West Coast. Her husband's a teacher so they don't have much money and airfare's expensive for the five of them. I haven't seen the new baby yet and he's nine months old."

"Then those pictures were important to you."

"Well . . . yes, but I'm sure my daughter will send me copies. It's all right, Mr. Speer."

"I'd like to replace your pictures, Helen. We have an excellent photographer right here at the hotel. Could you and your husband stay for another week?"

Helen glanced at her husband and he nodded.

"Good." Mike grinned. "Why don't you call your

daughter and tell her the Speer Palace invites her to be our guest for a week's vacation. That includes the whole family, of course. We can't replace those pictures unless your daughter's husband and children are here."

"You'll pay the airfare and everything?" Roger Burkholtz looked stunned. "But, Mr. Speer! You don't have to go to all that trouble."

"It's no trouble, believe me. I want you to leave the Speer Palace with good memories of your stay here. Go ahead, Helen. You can use my phone."

Mike got up and offered his chair to Helen. She sat down and dialed with fingers that shook a little. Mike smiled as he heard the beginning of her conversation.

"Hello, Peggy? No, nothing's wrong, dear. The most wonderful thing just happened. I got mugged!"

Gina poured a glass of champagne and handed it to Amy. "We might as well drink this before it goes flat. Mike and Jack won't be back for at least an hour."

"Go ahead, Gina. I've had more than enough. Mike's probably never going to let me drink champagne again."

"Oh?" There was a questioning look on Gina's face.

Amy sighed and gave in. It was just like Fairview again—she'd never been able to hold anything back from Gina.

"I had a couple more glasses of champagne after you left. Then, when Mike came back, I suggested we take a dip in the Jacuzzi. That's where we were when you called. I was . . . well . . . I wasn't wearing a bathing suit."

"Aha!" Gina laughed. "Seductus interruptus, right?"

That did it. Amy started to laugh, suddenly feeling much better.

"It took me five years to get this far and now that Mike's had time to think about things, he's probably going to avoid me for another five."

"That might be difficult." Gina grinned at her. "Don't forget that you're living with him now."

Mike leaned back in his chair and sighed. It was past one in the morning and everything had worked out just fine. Carole and Mel Schuman wouldn't say anything about the elevator mugging. They were too happy with the free weekend he'd given them and the diamond pendant. Helen and Roger Burkholtz certainly wouldn't complain about the security at the Speer Palace. And Donna was delighted with the bonus. Lucky they were all such nice folks.

"Damn!" Mike slammed his fist down on the desk. There would be no bad press but what would they try next?

Mike deliberately relaxed his clenched fist. He was upset about the mugging but he was even more upset at what had happened earlier. If it hadn't been for that well-timed phone call . . . There would be no more late-night dips with Amy. Mike wasn't sure what had gotten into him tonight but he'd damned near lost control. Sure, she'd deliberately provoked him by climbing in the Jacuzzi nude, but he should have had enough sense for both of them.

There was a knock on the door and Jack came in, followed by Mike's shoeshine man, Jake. "Mr. Patterson says he saw the two men as they got on the elevator. I thought you'd want to talk to him."

"Have a seat, Jake." Mike smiled to put him at ease. "Can you give us a description?"

Jake looked nervous. "Well, they were just ordinary-looking men, Mr. Speer. One was about as tall as I am, sandy-colored hair and a brown suit. The other one was bigger, about Mr. Humphries's size. He had darker hair and I think he was wearing a tweed jacket. I didn't really notice their faces, Mr. Speer. I'm really sorry."

"That's all right, Jake. Do you remember seeing them in the hotel before?"

"Nope. And I never polished their shoes, either."

"Their shoes?" Mike started to grin. "Tell me about their shoes, Jake."

Jake nodded. Now he was on familiar ground. "The smaller guy was wearing a pair of J.C. Penney deck shoes, about a year old from the looks of the soles. The stitching was ripped on both toes. I could tell they'd never been polished."

"How about the other man?"

"Now, his shoes were interesting. There was a three-inch lift in the right one but nothing in the left. They were brown Nunn-Bush dress shoes, customized at Wally's Ortho-Ped on Main Street. Wally's a friend of mine. I'd recognize his work anywhere."

"Thanks, Jake. You've been a big help." Mike slipped a bill in Jake's hand and showed him to the door. "I'm glad you were working on the third floor tonight."

Jack turned to Mike when they were alone again. "That was brilliant, Mike. I never thought to ask him about the shoes. I'll go down to Wally's Ortho-Ped in the morning and see what I can turn up."

"Sounds good." Mike stood up and stretched. "Let's

make a quick round of the floor. Gina and Amy are probably sleeping by now and I've got to unwind before I go up to bed."

"Francine's Folly?" Jack's mouth dropped open and he stared at Valerie Jeffries in amazement. "You're putting us on, Valerie. That was the hottest blue movie of the sixties. I saw it four times and Francine was a redhead."

Valerie laughed as Mike reached out to refill her champagne glass. "I wore a wig. It was the only thing I was allowed to wear in the whole damn movie. Ask Maxine. She played Denise, the French maid."

"No!" Both Mike and Jack looked amazed but Valerie's friend, Maxine Edwards, nodded solemnly. "Mademoiselle Francine always tells ze truth."

"She was the maid, all right." Mike lifted his glass and saluted Maxine. "I'd recognize that phony French accent anywhere."

When Mike and Jack had passed through the Dome Room on their nightly rounds, Valerie had spotted them and introduced her friend. Now they were all sitting around Mike's booth working their way through a second bottle of Dom Pérignon. "I've got a wonderful idea!" Maxine ran one gold-tipped nail over the back of Jack's hand. "Let's all go up to Valerie's suite and critique the movie."

"You've got it with you?" Mike raised his eyebrows and Valerie laughed. Her voice was throaty as she replied, "No, but I think we can remember our lines well enough for a second performance."

Mike and Jack stood by the bed as Maxine undressed Valerie. They'd done some wild things while they were at Thorton but there had been nothing to compare to this. Both of them felt like they were teenagers again, watching a scene in the movie they'd both sneaked in to see.

"Mademoiselle is zo hot and tired. Let Denise take off zese clothes zo she can relax on ze bed."

Maxine unzipped Valerie's dress and drew it off over her head. Mike and Jack gasped as they saw she was nude under her dress.

"Zat's zo much better." Maxine's fingers slid over the smooth skin of Valerie's back and moved around her body to brush against her breasts. Both men could see Valerie's nipples harden.

"And now, mademoiselle . . . to bed. Denise will turn down ze covers for you." Maxine bent low over the bed, folding back the sheets. She had nothing on under the short dress she wore and her buttocks gleamed in the light from the lamp.

Valerie sat on the edge of the bed, gazing up into Maxine's eyes. "I'm lonely, Denise. Pierre is gone and the thought of going to bed alone makes me sad."

"Zen Denise will go to bed with mademoiselle. Mademoiselle will zee how Denise can make her forget her lover."

"Denise! What do you mean?"

"Zis, mademoiselle!"

Maxine tossed off her dress and climbed on the bed. She reached out to caress Valerie's breasts and flicked her nails over the rosy nipples. "Can Pierre make you feel zis way? Can he make your whole body tremble with dezire?"

Valerie moaned and Maxine bent down. Valerie's moans grew louder as Maxine lapped at the sides of her breasts and traced a trail of gleaming wetness between the firm peaks. Mike was amazed. He'd watched two women making love before but something about seeing this movie scene reenacted made it much more exciting. He glanced quickly at Jack and saw that he wasn't alone in his fascination. They were both mesmerized by the sight of Maxine's bobbing head and the wet sounds she was making.

"More, Denise . . . I want more!" Valerie tried to push her friend's head down lower but Maxine looked up with a knowing smile. "Not yet, mademoiselle. First, you must kiss Denise as Denise kissed you. Zee how my breasts stand up and beg for ze touch of your lips?"

"But, Denise . . . I've never . . . Oh!"

Valerie's protest ended in a groan as Maxine bent down and rubbed her nipples over Valerie's lips. Valerie hesitated for a moment, a confused expression on her face, and then her mouth opened eagerly. There was a long pause, punctuated only by sighs and moans. Then Maxine swiveled around on the bed and spread Valerie's legs widely.

Mike drew in his breath. This particular scene in the movie had fueled his fantasies for months, but it was infinitely more exciting knowing that he could reach out and touch that glistening pink valley.

Maxine's dark head bent down and she pursed her lips. Her tongue flickered out and lapped expertly. Valerie squealed and shuddered as Maxine buried her head between Valerie's thighs. "Oh, yes!" Valerie groaned, pulling Maxine's body toward hers. "Come closer, Denise. I want you, too."

For a moment both Mike and Jack stood immobile, watching. Then Mike nudged Jack and pointed at the bed.

"But . . . but we're not through with the scene!" Valerie protested as Jack lifted Maxine up in his arms and carried her off to the other bedroom.

"I know how actresses hate to be interrupted." Mike reached down to the wetness between her legs. "Let's see if we can finish this scene all by ourselves."

14

IT WAS EASY to see that Vince Petrelli wasn't happy. He sat behind his chrome and glass desk in his high-tech office in Chicago's Loop and glared at the two men who faced him.

"There's nothing in this paper about the mugging!"

The two men exchanged nervous glances. They had discussed all this on the plane from Chicago. The tall man had argued for being apologetic, for begging forgiveness, but his sandy-haired partner had convinced him to hold his tongue.

"We followed our instructions to the letter, Mr. Petrelli. We got on the first elevator that wasn't covered. The stuff we took is right here."

Vince scowled as he opened the briefcase and dumped it out on his desk. There was nothing but a cheap pendant, three women's purses, a pair of earrings and a wallet. "It's a bunch of shit. You should have picked a better target."

"But, Mr. Petrelli . . . we were only following our orders."

"Get out of here! You don't even have the brains to pull off a grab and run." The two men exchanged another glance and scurried toward the door, happy to be leaving Petrelli's office in one piece.

Vince snorted disgustedly and dumped the contents of the briefcase in the trash. What a break for Speer.

Vince thought about his other plans for the casino. Things would be a lot easier if he could just hit Speer and be through with it. He'd been setting up his inside man for months now and the little bastard would hand over Speer's private elevator code with no trouble at all. The blonde had moved in with Speer and Vince had heard that she was a looker, which made the whole prospect even more exciting. A cruel smile played over Vince's face as he thought about the treat in store for him. He'd make Speer suffer for holding out so long.

There was only one thing keeping Mike Speer alive. He was Claudio's godson, and if a Petrelli godson turned up dead, Claudio would be honor-bound to track down the killer. Vince couldn't take that chance right now. Better to wait until the old alliances no longer applied.

There was something he could do right now to make up for his frustration. He still had some of his mother's money left and he had a perfect way to use it. Vince picked up the phone. "Ray? This is Vince. There's a couple of third-rate free-lancers leaving the building right now. They need to learn it doesn't pay to take my money and then fuck up the action. Make sure the lesson is painful. And Ray? When you're done, get your ass up here. I've got another job that's right up your alley."

Vince smiled. There was no way Mike Speer could keep the next attempt out of the papers, especially if a couple of his guests got themselves killed. Vince had a plan that would finish him off for good.

Vince reached down and rubbed his crotch, thinking of Speer's classy blonde. "Oh, Ray? One more thing.

You know that new secretary we just hired? The young one with the tits? Send her up right away. I just started something I want her to finish."

Mike rolled over in his king-size bed and groaned as he reached out to shut the alarm off. He vaguely remembered hearing Amy and Gina leave at some ungodly hour, not long after he'd gotten to bed. Pulling open the drapes, Mike blinked in the glare from the midmorning sun. He'd come back to his apartment at five in the morning and let himself in as quietly as he could, telling himself he was just being considerate. There was absolutely no reason to feel guilty about his adventures with Valerie and Maxine.

After a quick cold shower, Mike felt halfway human. He had thirty minutes to get dressed and Jack had cautioned him about his appearance. Jessie, Jack's snitch, would clam up immediately if he guessed that Mike owned the Speer Palace. For the Rolex his father had given him Mike substituted a Timex he'd picked up at the gift shop. Then he put on the worn blue jeans he'd meant to give to the Salvation Army and a dark-green knit shirt that had seen better days. They were meeting Jessie downtown, at a bar called the Dew Drop Inn.

Mike wandered into the kitchen and poured himself a cup of leftover coffee. Gina must have made it. Flip had mentioned that Amy's cooking skills were nonexistent and, now that he thought about it, Mike was sure Chef Sussman had mixed up his birthday cake. Amy'd said she had *baked* it.

The phone rang as Mike took his first sip. Jack had checked out Wally's Ortho-Ped this morning and come up with a name, John Green, who had paid for Wally's services in cash. There was no way to trace him, and the name was probably a fake, anyway. The elevator mugging looked like a professional job with help from the inside. The schedule for Mike's roving security guards was changed every three days but Mr. Green and his accomplice had still zeroed in on an unprotected car. Jake had remembered seeing them pass up the first and second elevators that had stopped when the man with the deck shoes deliberately dropped some change on the floor.

Mike carried his mug out on the patio and sat down at the picnic table. There was another new hotel going up in the next block and he could hear the faint sound of hammering and a rhythmic beeping as some piece of heavy equipment backed up. Then there was the sharp blast of a whistle and all the construction sounds ceased as the workers took their lunch break.

The thermometer hanging over the redwood lanai read eighty-six degrees in the shade. Usually he could count on a nice sea breeze, but not today.

It was almost time to meet Jack. Mike glanced up at the moosehead as he headed back to the kitchen and did an abrupt double take. There was a note stuck to the antlers, written on a Speer Palace memo blank.

To: Mike Speer. From: R. Moose. Subject: Privacy. Hey, Boss. Don't forget to unplug that damn phone tonight. I think she's going for the yellow rose. Your friend, Roscoe.

Mike couldn't help laughing, but he sobered quickly when he realized he had a real problem on his hands. He'd hoped that Amy's boldness last night was due to champagne but she must have been clear-headed this morning. His escapade with Valerie and Maxine had been a deliberate attempt to take his mind off Amy. Through bitter experience, Mike had learned that affairs starting on the rebound almost always ended badly. There would be no way Amy could continue to work closely with him, and he'd lose both a valuable employee and her friendship for good. As casino people were fond of saying, the percentages were wrong.

His coffee was growing cold but Mike took a gulp anyway as he tried to consider the whole thing in a positive light. Amy was twenty-three years old and hardly a blushing virgin. She'd had one affair that he knew of and probably several others. Also, she never jumped into things without thinking them over carefully, first. He had the note to prove her desire, and it was certainly mutual.

Mike began to smile as he remembered how Amy's breasts had glistened in the moonlight, the passionate response of her lips. But did she really know what she was doing? Mike folded the note and stuck it in his pocket. He'd figure out what to do later. Right now he was late for his meeting with Jack. As he rode down, he wondered how Amy had found out about the yellow roses.

Vince's hands shook slightly as he pulled up the circular driveway and parked his Jaguar in the garage. Claudio had called within minutes of arriving home and ordered Vince to meet him immediately. Vince knew why: Gina was still missing and Vince's men hadn't found a trace of her.

"Hello, Papa." Vince tried to smile but his palms started to sweat the moment he saw his father. Claudio's face was a thundercloud of displeasure and Vince knew he was literally a dead man if his father ever found out the truth.

"Shut the door!"

Vince closed the door and stood there warily. His father waved him toward a chair. "Sit!"

Vince obeyed hastily while his mind raced to figure out the best way out of the mess. The old wooden clock that had belonged to his grandfather ticked loudly in the silence and he jumped as it chimed the hour. His nerves had gone to pieces.

Claudio glared at Vince. "You were the last person to see Gina. What did she say?"

"Nothing, Papa . . . just like I told you over the phone. We only talked for a couple of minutes and then I left. When I came back later, Gina was gone."

"Lies!" Claudio's dark eyes were merciless as he confronted his son. "You had two men out looking for Gina before midnight last night. You *knew* she'd run away!" Vince winced as his father pounded his fist on the desk. There was a leak in his organization somewhere but he didn't have time to worry about that now.

"I didn't know, Papa. Honest. I just thought maybe she was upset . . ." Vince took a deep breath, ". . . at me."

"What?!" Claudio's voice was a bellow of rage and Vince started talking, fast.

"Just like I told you, Gina was out on the patio when I came home. She was sleeping and her bathing suit had kind of pulled up . . ."

Claudio banged his fist on the desk again, so hard that Vince jumped. "If you laid one finger on my—"

"Wait a second, Papa, I'll tell you everything. I admit I watched her for a while, thinking about what a good wife she'd make. You know I've always liked Gina. Then she woke up and I kissed her. I was going to ask her to marry me but . . . well . . . she got all upset and ran up to her room."

"You're an idiot, Vince. A girl like Gina you don't approach like some kind of a *puttana!*"

"I realize that now, Papa. She must have thought I was acting fresh or something and she didn't even give me a chance to propose. I figured the best thing I could do was leave. I really didn't mean to scare her, Papa. I wouldn't scare Gina for anything."

"You want to marry Gina?" Claudio's icy stare thawed just a bit.

"Sure, Papa, like I said. I was going to ask her when . . ."

Claudio began to smile. "Shut up, Vince, and don't spoil it. Without knowing it, you've given me the best news I could ask for. My little Gina's going to become a Petrelli at last. We'll announce your engagement just as soon as we find her."

A dive left over from the forties, the Dew Drop Inn offered a scarred wooden bar with a mirror behind it and an overpowering odor of stale beer. An older man in a brown work uniform stood by the end of the bar with one foot propped up on the rail. His name, Rodney, was sewn on a patch over his right pocket and the back of his shirt claimed he worked for the Di-Dee Diaper Service.

Right at home, Jack walked up to the bar, with Mike following a pace behind. "How's it going, Ed? Is Jessie here?"

The bartender, a sad-looking man with bushy eyebrows and a dirty white apron, nodded toward a table in the back. The five-dollar bill Jack had laid on the bar was slipped into the bartender's pocket with a smile so fleeting that Mike wondered if he had imagined it.

"Lots of local color in here." Jack gestured toward a booth in the corner where five construction workers, still wearing their hard hats, were telling jokes.

"So she gives him this nasty look and then she says, 'Crunch-Bird, my ass!'" pronounced a beefy black guy. All five cracked up, including the one who had told the joke, and Mike couldn't help wishing that he'd heard the whole thing.

Jack led Mike past another booth where an overdressed man in a white linen suit complete with a Panama hat was sitting with a girl who looked no more than fifteen years old. She was wearing a purple rayon blouse that was stained under the arms. As Mike approached, she looked up at him pathetically. The man slipped out of the booth and went to the men's room. Mike hesitated, tempted to ask if he could help, but Jack propelled him past the booth. "Keep moving. It's a setup. Some bozo feels sorry for her and plays the hero. She's so grateful she takes him up to her room, the pimp shows up, they roll the guy, and he's too embarrassed to report it."

Mike spotted Jessie in a booth at the back. He was a skinny white guy in his twenties with acne-scarred skin and lank brown hair that hadn't seen a barber's shears in at least two years. His dirty polyester shirt in a bright orange paisley print looked like it dated from the early sixties and hadn't been washed since then. Despite the solid wall at his back, he looked as nervous as hell.

"Hey, Jessie." Jack slid into the booth. "Meet my friend. He's interested in buying some information."

"You didn't say nothin' about a friend." The complaints stopped when Jack tucked a twenty under the ashtray.

"You're not going to disappoint us, are you, Jessie?"

"No, I got something but it was real hard to find out. People ain't talkin' much."

"That's what we're paying you for, Jessie." Jack slipped out another twenty and Jessie eyed the money greedily.

"I do a little work for the Cardinellas every once in a while. I heard they grabbed some woman night before last and left her in the dump. You wanna hear about that?" Jack nodded and added another twenty to the pile.

"It was Al and Roberto that did it. I heard 'em bragging the other night. They got orders from Cardinella himself but it wasn't for him. It was a favor for another family, a family from out of town."

"Which family?" Mike was insistent.

Jessie looked to Jack, indignant at Mike's violation of the unwritten rules. Jack laid a hand on Mike's forearm to warn him, then repeated the question. "Which family was it?"

Jessie waited until Jack put out another twenty before he started talking again. "This same family we're talking about was connected to that elevator thing at the Palace last night. I'm not sure I can remember the name. You know how it is when you get old."

"Maybe this'll bring it back." Jack added another twenty to the pile.

"Maybe it won't." Jessie looked up at Jack. "I got a lot to lose here. These people kill for fun. Why do you think I'm sitting here with my back against the wall? My nerves are shot."

"You might like to take a little vacation after you leave here, Jessie. You should relax those shot nerves. Here's another couple of bucks for bus fare." Jack added forty to the pile and Jesse nodded. Then he leaned close and lowered his voice to a whisper.

"It's the Petrellis. That's the straight scoop, Jack. The Petrellis are behind all this. They want to take over the Palace."

Jack nodded. "Okay, Jessie. This'll make it an even two big ones. There's more where this came from if you hear anything else. I'll be in touch."

Jack nodded to Mike and they stood up. Jessie was still eyeing the door nervously. Mike leaned down close to Jessie and lowered his voice. "You ought to be more careful. There's an air-conditioning vent over your head. Remember what happened to Mugs Muretto."

"Mugs Muretto?" For a minute Jessie looked confused. "Oh, yeah . . . you're right. Thanks." Mike watched him eyeing the vent nervously until he was safely out the back door.

Jack waited until they got into the car. "All right. Who the hell is Mugs Muretto?"

Mike shrugged. "I don't know. I made it up. I figured it was what Jessie deserved for giving us a bum steer."

"We've got three leads pointing us straight to Chicago. R. D. Pierce's bank deposit, his airline trip, and Jessie's information. You still don't think it could be the Petrellis?"

"No way. I've got Claudio's word."

"Jesus!" Jack banged his fist on the wheel. "Don't give me that honor among thieves bullshit, Mike. Claudio Petrelli is a ruthless killer. Even the other dons are afraid of him."

"They respect him. That's not the same thing as

being afraid. Anyway, he wouldn't lie to me. I'm his godson."

"Claudio Petrelli's godson?" Jack's eyes widened. "And Jessie says the Petrellis are after you? Jesus, Mike. It's a good thing you're a friend of mine or I'd never have taken this case."

15

AMY SAT AT her desk and took notes as she listened to the man on the phone. It was the second time he'd called. "Certainly, Mr. Pierce. I'll be sure to give Mr. Speer your message. And you'll be at that number all day?"

Amy underlined the number as the man repeated it. It was another attempt to buy the Speer Palace by the same investment group. When Mr. Pierce had called last month, Mike had turned him down flat. Amy was frowning when she hung up the phone. She'd thought Mike and Jack had settled everything with Pierce yesterday.

"Miss Warner?" Amy's secretary stuck her head in the door. "The head waiter from the Dome Room called while you were on the other line. There's some trouble with the health inspector. I told him you'd come up just as soon as you could."

Amy groaned. Health inspections were made every month and they'd never had any trouble before. She hoped it was something she could handle quickly. She had a meeting with the housekeeping staff in less than an hour. "Thanks, Joyce. Hold down the fort here. I'm leaving right now."

Amy hurried down the hallway and onto the casino

floor. Business was brisk for a Monday afternoon. She noticed a large crowd around the blackjack tables. The delegates to the American Heart Association Convention had checked in this morning and most of them had headed for the tables to get in a little gambling before the opening speech at dinner. As she walked past the tables a man in a brown suit intercepted her.

"Excuse me. Miss Warner? We seem to have a small problem with the dinner menu." For a moment Amy went absolutely blank on the man's name. Then she remembered that he was president of the Heart Association and his name was almost a pun. Valentine. The man's name was Dr. Steven Valentine. "Yes, Dr. Valentine?"

"It's probably silly of me to worry but several of the delegates have expressed concern over the butter. They asked me to make sure it's a polyunsaturated margarine, either a corn oil or safflower oil spread will be fine."

"I'm just on my way to see Chef Sussman right now. I'll tell him."

"Thank you." The little doctor beamed. "Other than that, everything is perfect."

Amy breathed a sigh of relief, hoping the problem with the health inspection would be just as easy to solve.

Amy smiled at a couple on the elevator whose child was entranced by the view. As the door opened on the top floor, Amy reached in her pocket and handed the mother a guest courtesy card for free ice cream cones.

"Oh, thank you, but we're not guests here." The mother tried to hand back the card.

"That's all right." Amy smiled. "I'm sure your little boy would like a free ice cream cone."

Amy got off but the family stayed on, as most tourists did. Mike's liberal use of the courtesy cards was good policy. Even if that particular family never stayed at the Speer Palace, they would mention it to their friends.

There was a sign on the restaurant door. CLOSED BY ORDER OF THE BOARD OF HEALTH. Amy stared at it for a moment. There was no way the Speer Palace could stay in business without a first-class restaurant on the premises. She had to do something, fast.

Amy heard the commotion the moment she opened the kitchen door. Chef Sussman was obviously upset. His toque was askew and he paced across the kitchen floor furiously. All the waiters and busboys were staying well out of his way.

"I tell you my kitchen is clean! There's no way that cockamamie health inspector found mice droppings in my pantry!"

Amy rushed up to the enraged chef and took his arm. It was a little like hanging on to a cyclone. "Chef Sussman. Chef Sussman! Just calm down for a moment, please."

"Mice, schmice! He says we have to close until we fumigate. Fumigate for what? We put out traps. They're always empty. My busboys clean that pantry every day!"

"I know they do, Chef Sussman. I've seen them do it. Now, just calm down and think. Were you with the health inspector the whole time he was checking the pantry?"

Chef Sussman stopped his frantic pacing for a moment and stared at Amy. Then he smacked the palm of his hand against his head.

"Of course! I left him alone in the pantry to put the

dinner rolls in the oven. That must have been when he planted the evidence. Why didn't I think of that?"

"It's difficult to think clearly when you're upset." Amy patted the chef on the arm. "Now, why don't you show me exactly where the health inspector found the droppings."

Chef Sussman straightened his toque and led Amy to his pantry. He pulled out a crate and pointed.

"Right there!"

"Wait just a minute." Amy examined the crate. "These are jars of ripe olives. Mice can't get into sealed jars and they don't eat olives."

The chef nodded. "You're right. That proves the little momzer set us up. I was standing right next to him when he checked the flour and grains. He found nothing. If we really had mice, that's where the droppings would be."

"Mike should be back any minute." Amy glanced at her watch. "He can call the health board and request another inspection."

"That'll be too late." Chef Sussman sighed deeply. "Tonight is the banquet for the Heart Association."

"How about the kitchen in the coffee shop? I know that's asking a lot, but do you think you could prepare tonight's menu down there?"

The chef shook his head sadly. "You know I'd do anything to help Mr. Speer, but that's impossible. The coffee shop kitchen is short order only and the menu calls for roast beef. I can't prepare roast beef on a grill."

"There must be something we can do. If this gets out we'll never book another convention."

Chef Sussman snorted bitterly. "If I could get my hands on that health inspector, we could substitute long pig for the main course. I'd roast him over a spit with his badge in his mouth!"

Amy nodded. She knew exactly how the chef felt. With the kitchen closed there was no way they could hold the banquet tonight unless . . . "You've just given me an idea." Amy began to smile. "Could you roast the beef on a spit if we rig up some sort of barbecue pits?"

Chef Sussman smiled back. "It could be done. We could have a barbecue by the pool, just like they did when I was a child in the old country."

Amy couldn't help her look of surprise. "Which old country?"

"Los Angeles, but don't tell anyone. A chef must have a certain mystique. Everyone assumes Julia is French but she was born in California.

Amy laughed. "Your secret is safe with me, Chef Sussman."

The chef nodded and pulled a pad of paper out of his pocket. "We could make it a theme banquet. Perhaps a luau."

"Great. I'll arrange for garlands of flowers and Hawaiian music. Do you think we can pull it off in time?"

Chef Sussman glanced at his watch. "Yes, but we'll have to start right away."

"Order anything you need. I'll go down and see Fred at the flower shop. And I'll have someone give the dancers a crash course in the hula. We'll tell the Heart Association it's a party Mr. Speer planned especially for them. Oh, yes . . . make sure you use a polyunsaturated margarine. Dr. Valentine was concerned."

Chef Sussman gave Amy a harassed look but he nodded. He was already organizing his staff when Amy left the kitchen. She pressed the button for the elevator and sighed deeply. Another crisis was averted, at least temporarily, but now she was convinced that Mike was right. Someone was trying to put the Speer Palace out of business and they'd almost succeeded today. Amy didn't even want to think of what they might try next.

Mike was amazed at the way Amy had taken charge while he was gone. Twelve showgirls were being fitted for costumes and Gina was giving them hula lessons. Chef Sussman was out by the pool, marshaling his staff. Fred was draping garlands of tropical flowers over the trees near the pool and Amy had gone off to line up a band to play Hawaiian music.

Now Mike was on hold, waiting to talk to the chief health inspector. Jack made a thumbs up gesture when Mike was connected at last, listening in while Mike explained the problem. "Of course, sir." Mike's voice was properly subservient. "I understand your policy and I certainly approve. We don't want a health hazard at the Speer Palace, either." Mike doodled on his desk pad as he listened to the authoritarian voice on the other end of the line.

"I'm just requesting a second inspection, that's all. The kitchen's been sealed off and we'll keep it that way until you can send out another inspector." The pompous voice droned on. "A week?" Mike couldn't keep the shock out of his voice. "But we can't wait that long. It's critical!"

Jack reached for the desk pad, made a few marks, and handed it back to Mike. Mike glanced down at it. A huge dollar sign.

"I realize the problems you must have with scheduling but I'd be more than willing to pay for your overtime. Yes. Whatever you feel is fair." Jack nodded and drew an arrow pointing to the top of the page. Higher.

"And of course I'd take care of any other expenses you might incur in arranging a special inspection. I imagine there's a fee for things like that." Jack pointed to the dollar sign again and Mike nodded. He was getting the general idea.

"If you could come out tonight, sir, I'd be delighted to show you around. Your wife, too, of course. I'll assign one of my staff to make sure she has a good time while you're doing the inspection. There's a wonderful little boutique downstairs and a first-class jewelry store."

The voice on the other end of the line droned on and Mike sighed. He was running out of nice ways to offer money. "Oh, I see, sir. Of course I wouldn't feel right asking you to delay your vacation unless I could offer some sort of compensation. We have our own travel bureau right here at the hotel. Why don't you call and cancel your tickets? We'll be glad to make new reservations for you."

Jack grinned as Mike clinched the deal. A Speer Palace limo would pick up the health inspector and his wife at six this evening. Naturally they'd stay for dinner and drinks the moment the Dome Room Restaurant was reopened. Mike had even offered a guest suite for the night, just in case the inspector's wife wanted to take in the show. "Jesus, I'm glad that's over!" Mike hung up the phone with relief and Jack reached out to shake his hand.

"You did just fine. I don't think it'll cost you more than a couple of thousand to get your restaurant open again. Dealing with a scumbag like that's a pain, isn't it?"

"It's frustrating. Why didn't he just name his price? I would have paid it."

Jack looked stunned. "A city official taking a cash bribe? He wouldn't dare do that. It's illegal!"

Jack whistled as he rode across town in the Speer Palace limousine. Mike had given him carte blanche with R. D. Pierce and Jack found it even better than having the power of the pen that entitled trusted casino executives to sign chits for free meals, complimentary rooms, and unlimited credit.

The valet parker raised the gate to the parking lot and stood watching as the silver stretch limo with the Speer International emblem turned around. From his expression, Jack could tell he was impressed. Despite the fact that anyone could rent a limo for fifty dollars an hour, people always treated limo riders with respect and answered questions that would have raised eyebrows from anyone else. As Jack walked toward the Pierce Towers, he noticed that the limo driver was deep in conversation with the valet parker. Jack had spent the ride over coaching the man, and it looked like it might pay off.

This time Jack barged straight into R. D. Pierce's executive office. "Richard!" Jack dropped into a gray leather chair without being asked. "Now, what was all that bullshit on the phone?"

R. D. Pierce jumped up from behind his desk, his face the unbecoming shade of a Tobasco bottle. "You have no right to barge in here! I have appointments!"

"You have shit." Jack smiled and leaned back, crossing his legs. Lowell Chapman, the bank president, had told Mike that R. D. Pierce despised vulgarity. "Now, about that offer you made Mr. Speer this afternoon . . . tell Petrelli if he can't do better than that, he'd better roll his money in a ball and stick it up your asshole."

For a moment R. D. Pierce was so furious he just sputtered. Then he managed to force out his words. "Rest assured I'll tell Mr. Petrelli *exactly* what you said. Now, get out of my office! And don't come back!"

"Thank you for the information, Mr. Pierce." Jack got up and headed for the door. "I thought we were dealing with Petrelli but I didn't know for sure until you confirmed it just now."

R. D. Pierce's face lost its color so rapidly it was pasty white by the time Jack had crossed the room. Jack knew there would be no phone calls to Chicago. R. D. Pierce had recalled what the Petrellis did to informers.

"What happened?" Colleen came down the hallway at a dead run. "I heard Mr. Pierce shouting."

Jack shrugged. "I'm not sure but I think he's worried about his health."

Flip straightened his tie and took a deep breath before he walked into Amy's office. "Hi, Joyce. Is my sister in?"

Joyce Benson looked up from the letter she was typing, shoved her glasses back up her nose, and gave Flip a harassed look. "She's in but she told me she doesn't want to be disturbed. She's on the phone, two lines at once. It's been a madhouse here all afternoon." She guarded Amy's privacy like a mother lion defending her cub but Flip knew Joyce couldn't resist him for long. "I'll only take a second of her time, promise. I'll be so fast, she won't even remember she saw me."

Joyce laughed. "Oh . . . all right." She handed Flip the letter she'd just finished typing. "Take this in with you and tell her I can get it in today's mail if she signs it right away."

Amy looked up and gave a wave as Flip came in the door. "That's fine, Bill. I've got Sam on the other line right now and I'll connect you. Work out the arrangements between the two of you and be here at six o'clock tonight." Flip watched the telephone console as Amy pushed a switch to connect the two flashing buttons. A second later they both glowed brightly. He assumed that meant Bill and Sam were talking to each other.

"Hi, Flip. What a day!" Amy sighed and reached for her coffee cup.

Flip pushed the letter across Amy's cluttered desk and handed her a pen. "Joyce said if you sign this now, she can mail it today."

"Done!" Amy scribbled her name and handed it back. "What brings you down here?"

Flip took the letter and folded it carefully. "Money. I hate to ask you, but I'm a little short this week."

"No problem, I'm a little long." Amy laughed and handed Flip some money. "I don't have to pay my rent this month, thanks to Mike."

"I've been meaning to talk to you about that. You're not looking for another apartment, are you?"

Amy shrugged. "Joyce mentioned that there's a vacancy in her building but I haven't really decided what to do yet."

"Good!" Flip looked relieved. "Don't even bother to look for an apartment. I want you to stay with Mike."

"But Mike might have other ideas. What if he doesn't want me to stay?"

"He does. I'm going to see him next and I'll make sure of it. Now, promise me you'll stay with Mike. It's a lot safer!"

"All right, I promise. I'll stay just as long as I'm welcome."

Amy frowned as the door closed behind Flip. Something was bothering her brother. Flip had always been concerned about her safety but this time he was going overboard. And what was this sudden need for money? She knew Flip's salary to the penny and there was no reason he should run short. Amy made up her mind to arrange an uninterrupted evening with Flip just as soon as she could.

"Mike? Got a minute?" Flip rushed into Mike's office and flopped down in one of the white leather chairs in front of his desk. "I've only got a few seconds but I wanted to talk to you. It's about you and Amy living together."

Mike sighed. He'd been putting this off but now the time was right to make sure Flip understood the situation. "I've been meaning to talk to you, too. Look, Flip, as far as Amy and I are concerned—"

"I just came from Amy's office. Living upstairs really seems to agree with her. You two are getting along all right, aren't you?"

"Sure. But, I want to make it clear that Amy and I—"

"You like Amy, don't you, Mike?"

"Of course I do!"

"And you want her to live with you, don't you?"

"Of course, but—"

"Good! I hope you two decide to stay together for a long time."

"Wait a second, Flip. Amy and I . . . well . . . as far as our sleeping arrangements—"

"Hold it, Mike. I didn't come in here to pry into

something that's really none of my business. I just wanted to tell you that I think it's great that my sister's living with you." Flip got up and headed for the door. "Now I've got to run. I have a meeting in five minutes."

Flip was gone before Mike could close his mouth. Mike stared at the door for a second and then he shook his head. Flip assumed that he was sleeping with Amy and he wasn't a bit upset.

Mike laughed out loud as he realized he'd been an incredible fool. The hotel staff approved. Their friends approved. Amy's brother approved. And Amy had even left him an invitation. Why was he dragging his heels? Amy would be going upstairs to dress for the luau in less than an hour and he had to get there first to leave her a note. No wonder she'd given him Roscoe for his birthday. That moose made a great cupid.

16

JERRY KLEIN LOOKED up as Mr. Nichols, Room 213, walked past the open doorway. He'd learned that the tips were much better if he called the guests by name.

The desk in the room next door was piled high with psych textbooks, most of them bristling with markers and marginal notations. He was a sophomore at J.C. State, working to put himself through school. Mr. Speer had given him permission to study in any vacant room and Jerry's only responsibility was to come running when the front desk rang for him.

It was quiet over the dinner hour tonight and Jerry was grateful. He'd ace his test tomorrow, as usual. His photographic memory was a definite asset but he never relied on it entirely, putting in all the study time he could spare. Mr. Speer was interested in his progress and had promised Jerry a job in management when he graduated.

The phone rang: more ice for the newlyweds, Jack and Lois Stowe, in Room 430. They were nice, friendly people from Minneapolis. Mr. Stowe had asked about fishing and Jerry had made a quick stop at the Speer Palace travel bureau to pick up schedules for the local charter boats. He stuffed them into his pocket and hurried out the door with the ice bucket.

Mr. Nichols was unlocking his door. Jerry gave him a friendly smile as he hurried past but Mr. Nichols was an odd duck. His hands had trembled when he'd signed the register and he'd told Jerry he was staying only one night even though he was entitled to two for the price of one. He'd also insisted on carrying his own suitcase and looked positively alarmed when Jerry had made a move toward it.

Jerry had tried to start a conversation when he had shown Mr. Nichols to his room, but the man hadn't said more than five words, a regular Calvin Coolidge. Most guests welcomed the opportunity to chat with a friendly bellboy, especially if they were checking in alone.

A phrase from Konjoyan's article on the secretive personality flashed through Jerry's mind. He closed his eyes and saw the text, page ninety-five, paragraph three. *The secretive personality is often adept at repressing abnormal tendencies, however, they may emerge occasionally as observable phenomenon frequently disguised as "nervous habits." E.g., a facial tic or twitch, a trembling of the extremities, a drumming of the fingertips under stress, etc.* Mr. Nichols had drummed his fingertips on the desk as he waited for his reservation to be confirmed. Jerry hadn't noticed a facial tick but that was still two out of three.

Jerry remembered his professor's warning. Most first-time psych students tended to see psychotics all over the place and he knew that the difference between the normal and abnormal personality was only a matter of degree. Maybe Mr. Nichols was a perfectly normal guy who was under a lot of stress. Perhaps he was married and had arranged to meet a lover here at the Speer Palace. Or he might be a member of Gamblers' Anonymous who was testing himself by staying overnight at a casino. Jerry knew it was foolish to speculate but he intended to keep his eye on the room next door, just in case. He knew that the anonymity of a big hotel attracted some strange sorts of people.

Jerry filled the ice bucket and caught the elevator to the fourth floor. No more than a minute had passed since he'd taken the call. Mr. and Mrs. Stowe would be amazed at the prompt service, people always were. And they showed their gratitude in a way that Jerry could really appreciate. He had already saved enough for next quarter's tuition.

Amy looked in the mirror. She was ready. The dress, a Hawaiian print that her dad and Rita had brought her from Honolulu, was perfect for a luau. The top was nothing more than a bikini top, printed with wild blue and white flowers; the skirt was a piece of the same material, cut to wrap around the waist. It was really quite modest, as long as there wasn't a strong breeze.

Fred had given her a white hibiscus, explaining that a flower worn on the right side meant that the woman was married. A flower on the left signified that the lady would be receptive to a man's advances. Amy chuckled as she recalled Fred's warning: *Be sure to wear it on the right side, Amy. Mr. Speer knows the custom.*

But, Fred. You know I'm not married.

That's true, but this custom's kept pace with the times. A flower on the right also means that you're engaged for the evening with a special friend.

Amy laughed as she picked up the flower and deliberately tucked it behind her left ear. Fred would be shocked but she had to do something. Mike hadn't reacted at all to her note from Roscoe.

There was a plaintive meow at her feet and Amy bent

down to pet Katy. She was probably hungry again. Katy had done nothing but eat and nap in the sun since they'd moved into Mike's suite, obviously contented with their new living arrangements.

"Come on, Katy. I'll feed you." Amy walked to the kitchen, Katy at her heels. The first thing she saw was Mike's jacket, draped over the back of a chair. Mike must have come up to the suite this afternoon.

Heart pounding, Amy raced to the patio, ignoring Katy's protesting yowl as her mistress bypassed the food bowl. There was a note stuck on Roscoe's antlers. Amy's heart pounded as she climbed up on a stool.

To: Amy Warner. From: R. Moose. Subject: Thick-headedness. I think he's finally beginning to get your message. I'd chill the champagne, if I were you. Love, Roscoe.

Amy rushed back into the house and grabbed a bottle of champagne from Mike's wine rack. Chill the champagne? You bet she would! The little calico brushed up against Amy's skirt and gave a heart-rending meow as she eyed the cartons of cream in the fridge.

"All right, Katy. You'll get your cream." Katy made a dive for the cream as Amy set it down. If she didn't know better, Amy would have sworn the little cat hadn't eaten in a week.

In less than a minute the cream was half gone. Katy didn't even look up from her bowl as her mistress used the reflection in the patio door to switch the white flower from left ear to right.

* * *

Gina's hands fluttered through the air to spell out the story as her body moved sensuously to the Hawaiian beat. She still couldn't believe that she was out here in front of all these people, dressed in a grass skirt, leading a line of professional dancers in the hula. It was the one thing she'd learned at Fairview that had come in handy in later life.

A smile played over Gina's face as she remembered how it had come about. Before she'd left for the summer, Gina's faculty adviser had insisted she sign up for an additional course in physical education. Gina had forgotten all about it and in the fall the damage had been done: she found herself arbitrarily assigned to a semester of rock climbing. Gina was terrified of heights. On planes, she took the aisle seat just to avoid looking out the window. Even the thought of climbing a step stool made her break out in a cold sweat.

Frantically Gina had searched for another class. Amy's fencing class had been filled, as were girls' basketball, tennis, and volleyball. The only class that was still open had been a course in Hawaiian dance. Gina had spent three hours a week in the Fairview gym, practicing the hula, never dreaming that one day the practice would pay off.

Gina's eyes scanned the crowd. Jack had promised to meet her but she couldn't spot him in the mass of people surrounding the barbecue pits. Perhaps he had been delayed. Suddenly she noticed a man in the front row wearing the most awful Hawaiian shirt she'd ever seen. The beacon waved and Gina laughed out loud. Purple with day-glow yellow flowers, his shirt was blinding even in the dim light of the flickering torches.

The number ended and Gina stepped down from the

improvised stage. Jack was waiting. "That was fantastic, Gina. Will you teach me? I'm dressed like a native."

Gina bit back a smart retort and hooked her arm through his. The shirt was polyester, made in Taiwan, but Jack looked handsome in anything he wore.

The man who had signed in as Mr. Nichols pulled aside the corner of the drapes and glanced out his window at the huge crowd by the pool. Most of them appeared to be having a good time, and faint strains of Hawaiian music came through the closed window. The man frowned. His work took concentration and he would have preferred a quieter room, but his instructions had been to secure Room 213. He was paid good money to do exactly as he was told.

He hefted the heavy metal suitcase and placed it carefully on the bed. He was fond of the suitcase. It had brought him luck on three other occasions and he had no doubt that he'd use it again. His profession depended on good recommendations and this would be the most important job of his career.

There was a knock on the door and he went to answer it. It was probably that damn bellboy again, bringing his lemonade. The kid was really hustling for tips, knocking on his door without being summoned and asking if he could bring anything. It might be smart to stiff him on the tip so he'd knock it off.

"Here you go, Mr. Nichols." Jerry Klein came in with a tray and set it down on the dresser. "I brought you a roast beef sandwich from the luau. It's free."

"Yeah, thanks, kid. I'll catch you later, huh? All I got are big bills." The kid looked a little disappointed but he took the hint and left. The man locked the door, took a key from his pocket, and opened the suitcase. He had things to do before midnight.

The luau was still going strong at ten-thirty when Jack and Gina slipped away. Jack had suggested a stroll on the beach, so Gina changed to jeans and a bright red Speer Palace sweatshirt that Amy had given her. She shivered as they walked out onto the empty stretch of sand. Everyone else seemed to be inside the casinos and the beach had a desolate feel that would have scared Gina if she'd been alone.

"Are you cold, Gina?" Jack moved to put his arm around her.

"No!" Gina jerked away so fast she stumbled slightly on the uneven sand. When she turned to look at Jack there was a hurt expression on his face.

"I did it again." Gina sighed deeply. "I'm sorry, Jack. I guess I'm just touchy around men lately. Believe me, it has nothing to do with you personally."

Jack led her over to a high dune where they could be sheltered from the sea breeze. "Let's sit down, Gina. I think we need to talk."

Gina felt her mouth go dry as she sat in the lee of the dune. The casino lights glittered brightly against the dark sky in one direction and the moon glowed softly in the other. Nature versus technology. The neon lights appeared brighter but they wouldn't last for long if someone forgot to pay the power bill. The moon would shine softly forever.

"Listen to me, Gina. I'm no shrink but I know there's something wrong if you'd rather fall on your face than let me put my arm around you."

"I'm sorry, Jack. I just overreacted again, that's all. Really, it has nothing to do with you."

Jack nodded but Gina could tell he wasn't going to accept her simplified explanation. "Okay, I believe you. Now tell me why you overreacted and we'll try to work it out."

"I . . . I had a bad experience. With a man. That explains it, doesn't it?"

"It's a start. Now suppose you tell me all about it."

Gina fought back the urge to blurt out the whole thing. Jack would be sympathetic but she didn't even want to think about Vince, much less talk about him.

"This man, were you in love with him?" Jack prodded gently.

"No! I . . . I hate him!" Gina's eyes filled with tears. "I've always hated him!"

"But you don't feel that way about me, do you?"

"Oh, no, Jack! Of course I don't!"

"You're letting one experience color your whole attitude, Gina. I think it might help if you told me what happened. You can't keep it bottled up forever."

Gina gasped as he reached out and held her trembling hands tightly. He sat down next to her, their shoulders touching, and before she thought about what she was doing, Gina huddled up against him like a child. The story came out, in bits and pieces. Gina was crying too hard to be completely coherent but instinct warned her not to use any names. She knew Jack would hate the man who had hurt her and, although his methods might be different, he had the same drive for justice as Uncle Claudio.

"Oh, Gina. What a goddam shame!" Jack gathered her into his arms when she had finished at last, and Gina rested in his arms like a tired little girl, listening to the waves crash against the shore, feeling warm and secure for the first time since it had happened.

It was eleven o'clock, time for the first step. The man in 213 made sure the hallway was deserted and stepped out. They'd done him a favor by having that party outside. All the guests were out there, drinking free booze and eating free food. The hallway was completely empty.

He froze when he saw the light coming from the next room. Someone was sitting there with the door open. Cautiously the man moved forward until he could see inside. It was that damn bellboy again, sitting at the desk, reading. He'd be sure to look up if he heard a noise in the hall.

The man went back to his room and shut the door. He dialed the room serve number taped on the phone and the desk answered on the first ring. They were efficient at the Speer Palace. "I need that bellboy again. The same kid that brought my tray. Tell him I could sure go for another one of those roast beef sandwiches."

By pressing his ear to the wall, the man could hear the phone ring in the room next door and a second later the kid rushed out. It would take him at least five minutes to get the sandwich.

The man waited a couple of seconds and tried the corridor again. He worked rapidly, picking the lock on the silver panel at the end of the hallway with ease and going straight to the correct valve. The schematic he'd requested from the city planning office made everything simple. One twist with the special tool, a type of fitted wrench designed especially for this job that was hanging on the wall, and the valve was closed. Now the second floor was without sprinklers. The man stuffed the tool under his jacket and closed the panel, locking it up tightly. Even if, by some miracle, someone managed to get to the panel, they'd pay hell trying to turn the valve by hand.

A second or two later, the man was back in his room. He had barely enough time to dump the first untouched sandwich in the wastebasket before the anticipated knock came at his door. The kid was fast. "Here you go, Mr. Nichols. I brought another lemonade, too, just in case. That roast beef is great, isn't it?"

"Yeah. Guess I was hungrier than I thought. Thanks, kid. Here's something for your trouble."

"Thank *you*, Mr. Nichols." The kid looked down at the twenty in his hand with surprise. "If there's anything else I can get for you, just call the desk."

A second later he was gone, still excited at the size of the tip. The man smiled as he shut the door. Twenty bucks was a small price to pay for getting rid of a nosy bellboy. Now the kid would spend the rest of his shift bragging about the tip he'd made tonight and he would be free to carry out the rest of his plans.

17

"FEELING BETTER?" Jack helped Gina to her feet and they started to walk along the beach.

"Oh, yes!" Gina turned to smile at him and this time she didn't miss a step as he draped a friendly arm around her shoulders. "Tell me more about the Dew Drop Inn, Jack. Did you and Mike find out anything?"

"Yes and no." Jack frowned. "I don't know what to think. Jessie's always been straight with me before."

"What did he say?"

"He said Cardinella used two free-lancers to grab Amy and set up the elevator robbery as a favor to the Petrellis. He claims they're behind the whole thing, a scheme to take over the Speer Palace." Jack stopped to light a cigarette and Gina kept her face carefully neutral in the glare from his lighter. Thank goodness Jack didn't know that Claudio Petrelli was her uncle!

"There are a couple of other leads pointing straight to the Petrellis," said Jack, putting his arm around her shoulders again, "but of course Mike won't believe it. Mike swears Claudio Petrelli wouldn't lie to his own godson."

"His godson?" Gina's voice quavered slightly.

"Are you all right, Gina?"

"Oh . . . of course I am. I'm just . . . shocked, that's all. I didn't realize Mike was in this much trouble." All the while Gina was talking, her mind was spinning. Jack's information *had* to be wrong. "I want to know, Jack. Could Mike lose the Palace?"

"Mike can't hang on here more than another month."

"But I thought the Palace was doing so well!"

Jack sighed deeply. "Mike had problems before he even started building. Somebody bought up enough Speer International stock to get a couple of bastards on the board. Then, when Mike's father died, they tried to . . ."

Gina listened in silence as Jack chronicled the obstacles Mike had encountered. It had to be someone else, someone who was using the Petrelli name. Like . . . Vince! She remembered him bragging about some investments he'd made with Dixie's money.

When Jack finished, he sighed deeply. "I hope I'm wrong about the Petrellis, Gina. When they go after something, they usually get it."

The man in Room 213 took down the huge picture that covered the inside wall and plunged the point of his knife into the dry wall. There was a slight crunch but the kid had left a moment ago to answer more calls for room service. The man had placed three, using names he'd memorized when he'd signed the register. It would take the kid quite a while to find out that all three were fake.

In a matter of seconds the man had cut a jagged hole large enough to get at the studs behind the dry wall, relieved to see they were made of wood. The city planning office's blueprints were accurate, right down to the placement of the nails. Twenty minutes later the studs were soaked with gasoline. He put down the can and went to the bed to pull off the sheets. They were linen. The Speer Palace was a high-class place. Linen was a finer weave than cotton and it would resist the flame a little longer. That was all to the good. He wanted to be able to get out before the fire was discovered.

The sheets went into the hole between the walls after they were thoroughly soaked. Then he replaced the piece of drywall he'd removed, with a corner missing—for room to toss in a match.

The smell of gasoline was strong and the man opened his window slightly. A breeze would help and the fireproof curtains would hide the blaze for a while. By the time anyone spotted it, the fire would be out of control.

A door closed in the next room. Once the connecting wall went up, these two rooms would turn into a giant inferno. The kid would never get out in time. The arsonist thought about sending the kid on another bogus room service call. He'd been nice about bringing that first free sandwich. But after all, bellboys were expendable and in this business he couldn't afford to be charitable.

The phone rang next door, another room service call. This was the kid's lucky night. The fire would be going good by the time he came back.

Setting his suitcase by the door, the man took out a handful of kitchen matches, lit one, and let the rest catch fire. Then he poked them through the hole in the dry wall, grabbed his suitcase, and opened the door. There was a satisfying whoosh as the sheets caught. He stepped out into the hallway and the door locked behind him. Everything that gave his fire more time to spread was nice.

He took the stairs and moments later was outside, hailing a cab. He would have liked to stick around and watch the fun but he had a twelve-thirty plane to catch. Vince Petrelli was waiting. The man was standing in line, waiting to board his flight when he found a Speer Palace guest critique card in his pocket. Mr. Mike Speer thanked his guests in advance for taking the time to fill out the card. Their comments would help him to give better service. The man took out a pen and checked off the boxes. No, he couldn't suggest any ways to improve the service. Everything had been perfect, especially the room service. And yes, he'd certainly enjoyed his stay at the Speer Palace.

The Speer Palace Boutique was filled with unusual gift items and Jerry glanced around as he waited for his delivery to be wrapped. Every employee got a twenty percent discount and Jerry spotted several things his mother might like for her birthday. He had just about decided on a Monopoly set made entirely of chocolate when the saleswoman behind the counter called out to him.

"What's the matter, Jerry? You haven't made one wisecrack tonight."

"Sorry, Janice, just thinking, I guess. There's a really weird guy on the second floor. I can't figure him out."

"You're playing junior shrink again?" Janice laughed. "Okay, Jerry. I'll bite. What's so weird about this one?"

"He's a loner, about forty, not bad-looking, a real nervous type. I took him a sandwich and he stiffed me on the tip. Then he called for another one. I brought it and he tipped me ten bucks. Said the first one was delicious. I left, but not before I spotted the first sandwich deep-sixed in the wastebasket."

"That's weird, all right. Maybe he felt guilty because he stiffed you the first time and ordered another one as an excuse to make it up to you."

Jerry frowned. "I thought of that but it doesn't ring true. He could have just come next door and tipped me. He saw me sitting right there at the desk."

"You're using the room next to his?"

Jerry nodded.

"Okay . . . then maybe he wanted to get rid of you for a couple of minutes so he could do something you wouldn't notice. Or something you wouldn't overhear."

Jerry thought for a moment. Then, suddenly, all the pieces fit together, down to the funny smell when he'd returned to the room. "Oh, my God! Call Mr. Speer, Janice. Tell him to meet me at 213. Then send for security. And hurry!"

It was almost eleven-thirty before Mike and Amy finally managed to break away from the luau. The evening had been an unqualified success. The health inspector had reopened the Dome Room and Dr. Valentine had pulled Mike aside to confide that he was personally recommending the Speer Palace for next year's convention.

"We did it, Amy." Mike slipped his arm around her shoulders as they walked through the lobby toward the elevator. "Another crisis averted, thanks to your quick thinking. That luau was a stroke of genius."

"It was really Chef Sussman's idea."

"Sure it was." Mike grinned down at her. "Just like the moose note was Roscoe's idea."

Amy's heart beat fast as they took the elevator up to the top floor. She'd noticed the way Mike had been staring at her all evening and once, while they were dancing, he'd kissed her right in front of Flip and Jack. At last, it was going to happen.

Mike unlocked the door. "Just let me check in with Alice. I'll tell her to hold all my calls and then I'll open the champagne."

Amy nodded. All night she'd looked forward to being alone with Mike, but now that the moment was here she was suddenly nervous. "I'll just go slip into . . ." Amy caught herself on the brink of a tired cliché. "Into . . . something else."

She rushed to her bedroom and got out of her Hawaiian dress. She had seduced a few men and a few had seduced her but she'd been calmer about it. Amy assessed her reflection in the mirror. She wasn't Playboy Bunny material but Mike had seen her nude last night in the moonlight and he'd enjoyed the view. Of course moonlight was flattering, like any dim lighting. Perhaps she should hurry out to the living room, light a fire, and turn out the lights.

Amy's hands were shaking as she dabbed Pheromone behind her ears, under her breasts, and on her wrists. She added another dab to the insides of her thighs, just in case, and slipped into the blue silk lounging outfit she'd bought this afternoon at the boutique. Valerie Jeffries shopped at the boutique, too, but the saleswoman had assured Amy that she hadn't bought anything in blue silk.

The material caressed her skin and Amy tingled with

anticipation. She could hardly wait to see what sex with Mike would be like. Would he be masterful, ripping the silk from her body and throwing her on the couch in wild abandon? Or would he want to talk first, to make everything soft and comfortable and completely natural? Maybe both, one right after the other.

The living room was dark and there was a fire in the fireplace. Mike was way ahead of her.

"Amy?" Mike called out from the kitchen. "Have you ever heard the joke about the Crunch-Bird?"

Amy stopped in midstep and stared at the kitchen door. She couldn't believe that Mike was going to tell jokes at a time like this! "I don't think so." Amy hesitated for a moment, then gave in. "Go ahead, Mike. Tell it."

"I can't. I don't know it."

"What?"

"When Jack and I were downtown this afternoon, I overheard a punchline, and it's been driving me crazy ever since."

"So what is it?"

"Crunch-Bird, my ass."

Amy thought for a moment, reviewing all the jokes she could remember. "I can tell you the one about the parrot and the plumber but I've never heard a joke about a Crunch-Bird."

Amy heard the champagne cork pop in the kitchen and Mike came in, carrying two glasses and an ice bucket. He smiled down at her as he handed her the glass. "You look almost as gorgeous as you did last night. Is that outfit for me?"

Amy nodded. She didn't know how she could be shy after last night but her face felt hot and she knew she was blushing.

"To us." Mike touched the rim of his glass to hers. "And to Roscoe. I've really been a fool, Amy."

"Me, too. I should have thought to buy you a moosehead years ago."

Mike laughed. He let her take one sip of her champagne, then he took her glass and set it down on the end table.

"You can drink it later. Right now . . ."

Amy felt her uncertainty vanish as Mike kissed her. Suddenly the million and one little details she had to take care of in the morning seemed unimportant and she was straining against him, her nipples taut against the silky fabric. Mike reached down and slipped the silk off her shoulders. It fell to her waist and Amy trembled as his fingers explored her smooth skin.

"Please, Mike. Let me take this off." Amy was breathless. She reached down to slide out of her clothes but Mike was faster. He pushed her back against the couch pillows, holding her tightly.

"Not this time. Tonight I get to do the unwrapping."

Amy trembled as Mike slipped the blue silk down lower. It seemed to take him forever. She reached up and stroked his bare chest as he took off his shirt.

"Hurry, Mike . . . please!" Amy's voice was urgent and Mike crumpled up his multicolored Hawaiian shirt and dropped it, then his other clothing, on the chair.

Amy's supple body glowed in the firelight, rosy-tipped breasts, curves of smooth creamy skin. Her arms trembled as they reached out for him. Mike felt as if he'd been waiting forever.

"Amy . . . darling." Mike reached out for her just as the telephone rang.

"Son-of-a-bitch!"

Amy came to her senses first. "You'll have to answer that, Mike. Alice wouldn't call unless it was an emergency."

"Damn! I'm sorry, Amy."

Amy jumped up from the couch and raced for the bedroom. She dressed as fast as she could, slacks, a sweater, and an old pair of moccasins. The phone meant trouble and Mike would need her.

Jerry turned and raced for the stairs, seeing smoke pouring out of the cracks under both doors before he got halfway down the corridor. There was no time to wait for Mr. Speer or security.

The sprinkler panel was at the end of the hallway and Jerry sprinted the distance and grabbed at the handle, but it was locked up tight. He ran for the front desk, hoping this whole section of hallway wouldn't be in flames before he could get back. "I need the master key, quick!" Jerry grabbed it out of the startled bell captain's hand. The smoke rolled up in thick, black clouds as he raced back to the sprinkler panel.

Jerry had no idea how the sprinkling system worked but all the valves were horizontal except one. Jerry heaved at it but it wouldn't budge at all.

"I've got the tool, Jerry!" Mike Speer came down the hall at a dead run. "Go back to the front desk!"

Jerry had never disobeyed a direct command from his employer before but there was no way he could leave Mr. Speer alone and in danger. His legs shook with a combination of fear and adrenaline but he stood where he was and helped Mike attach the tool to the valve. A second later the sprinklers came on, along with the fire alarm.

Mike shouted, "Keep down low and run! If your clothes start to burn, roll!"

Jerry grabbed for Mike's arm. He wasn't taking any chances on losing Mr. Speer in this smoke. They dashed forward just as the flames shot out of 213 and turned the place they had been standing into a roaring inferno.

18

AMY PACED THE corridor outside the small infirmary next to the administrative offices on the ground floor.

The door opened at last and Mike and Jerry came out, accompanied by the staff physician, Dr. Bartleman. As Amy glanced anxiously at him, the doctor made a thumbs-up gesture. Amy threw her arms around Mike and held him so tightly the buttons on his shirt pressed into her chest. "When I saw you run down that hall, I thought I'd die!"

"Hey, it's all right, Amy." Mike kissed her quickly and drew back. "Come on, now. We've got a crisis on our hands and I need your help. Hank'll be here in a second. He's talking to the fire chief."

A moment later Hank came down the hall. "The damage is fairly minimal, Mr. Speer. The chief says the fire was easily contained, once you turned on the sprinklers. Only two rooms on the second floor were directly affected but he took the precaution of evacuating the north wings on both the second and the third floor."

Mike nodded as he ran a mental tally. More than a hundred guests had been evacuated. There was no way he could keep this quiet. "Does the chief agree that it's arson?"

Hank nodded. "He's pretty sure. They'll go in with axes just as soon as it cools."

"Okay, Hank. Let's get out to the lobby."

They heard the commotion as they opened the outside door to the lobby. There was a crowd of angry people around the reservation desk, one man in front shaking his fist at the desk clerk. Mike took in the situation at a glance.

"I'll take over at the desk. Amy, you start at the back of that line. Reassure them. Tell them our sprinkler system worked perfectly, there's absolutely no danger, and we'll move them to other rooms, if they prefer. And if anyone insists on leaving, make sure to refund the full price of their room, even if they came here on a coupon deal."

"Any special instructions for me, Mr. Speer?" Hank was waiting, notebook in hand.

"Brief Jack Humphries on the situation and tell him to get to the fire chief right away, He's to see if the chief'll give out a statement about the safety precautions here at the Palace. He'll know how to handle it. And tell him to ask Gina to come down to help Amy."

Hank scribbled a note. "Got it. Next?"

"Have one of your men get Flip down here on the double. Set up a spot for him right here near the lobby to handle the press and don't let any reporters in without identification. Your men can escort them to Flip."

"Anything else?"

Amy spoke up. "How about coffee or drinks or something for the people who were evacuated?"

"Good idea, but we can do better. Get a list from the desk, Amy, and identify the people who were evacuated. If they agree to stay, give them a chit for a meal and fifty dollars in chips to use in the casino while they're waiting to get back in their rooms."

"How about me, Mr. Speer?" Jerry spoke up. "The doc said I was fine and I want to help."

"Okay, Jerry. As of now, you're promoted to guest relations. First, get that list for Amy, then go down to wardrobe and find a tux that fits. You can take the evacuated guests up to the Dome Room for dinner and make sure they have a good time. You've got unlimited power of the pen for tonight. Any questions?"

Jerry, Amy, and Hank shook their heads.

"Okay . . . let's get at it."

Amy watched Mike for a moment as he moved purposefully through the crowd and took his place behind the desk. The man who had been waving his fist looked surprised as Mike shook his hand. A second later he was nodding in agreement. A moment more and a slight smile appeared on his face.

Suddenly Amy shivered. Two in one day. The health inspection had been serious but this attack could have been disastrous. If Jerry hadn't been on the ball, the Speer Palace might have gone up in flames.

"Are you all right, Miss Warner?" One of Hank's security men moved to her side.

Amy took a deep breath and nodded. This was no time to think about what might have happened. Mike was counting on her to help. "I'm fine." Amy fixed her face in a smile and moved off toward a group of displaced guests, trying not to think about what Mike's enemy might try next.

Flip had failed again tonight. He knew the only way out of his dilemma, but he got hung up, as always, with method. A gun was too messy; someone would have to clean it up and Flip couldn't do that to a total stranger. Jumping off a tall building was much preferable but Flip had a horror of falling all those stories to live his life out as a hopeless cripple. Slashing his wrists was too slow. He knew he'd chicken out and rush to a doctor before he had time to bleed to death. And pills were a woman's way. If he couldn't kill himself with courage, he didn't want to do it at all. Flip knew his dilemma was humorous. He could see how ridiculous he was being—that was part of the problem—but he was backed into a corner and there was no way out except death by his hand or someone else's. The latter was the subject of many sleepless nights. He knew how his enemy killed.

Now the gun and the vial of pills were back in his drawer, locked up against the maid's prying eyes and Flip was asleep at last. The light was on by the bed. Flip had found he could no longer sleep in the dark without seeing Mike's accusing eyes in his nightmares.

It was one in the morning when the phone rang. Flip's eyelids twitched. He was dreaming about the house at the shore that his father had rented for a summer vacation twenty years ago. The Mickey Mouse alarm clock Amy had given him for Christmas stood on the dresser by his single bed. Flip could see it clearly in his dream. Kid stuff, but he liked it anyway. He had to remember to buy her one. She always gave him what she really wanted for herself.

Flip reached out groggily and pushed Mickey's nose. It was summer vacation and he didn't have to get up early today. Later, he'd go out in the boat with Mike and they'd sail to the point. Maybe they'd even take Amy along, if she promised not to be a pest.

The alarm rang again and Flip reached out to shut it off. Hadn't he just done that? The Mickey Mouse clock didn't have a snooze alarm. At least he didn't think it did. Maybe he'd missed something by not reading the instructions. He was up now, pulling on his clothes in a hurry. Mike was probably awake and they'd have pancakes for breakfast. Rose, the family cook, always made pancakes when Mike was here. She put chocolate chips in the batter and they were delicious.

The alarm rang again. Flip stared at it hard. Something was wrong. It looked like . . .

The phone. This time Flip really woke up. He grabbed the phone with one hand and sat up.

"Hello? Yeah, Hank. What's up?" At first Flip couldn't believe what he was hearing but when Hank's words finally sunk in, he jumped out of bed and grabbed for his clothes.

Mike needed him right away. Flip raced for the stairs, smelling smoke as he passed the second floor landing.

Hank was waiting for him by the desk. Flip swallowed hard as he moved through the crowd. Someone could have been killed tonight.

It was three in the morning before they could assess the damage. The two rooms on the end of the second floor, 213 and 211, were completely gutted by the fire. There was slight smoke damage to one room on the floor above but everything else was all right. Most of the guests had been understanding. Some had requested new rooms but only six had actually left the hotel. Naturally, Mr. Nichols was nowhere to be found. Jack and a couple of the Speer Palace security guards were combing the airport and the bus station but not with very high hopes. Mike, Amy, Gina, and Jerry were sitting in the white leather chairs in Mike's office.

"Let me see if I've got everything, Jerry," said Mike, referring to his notes. "You said Mr. Nichols was about five-ten, brown hair, brown eyes, approximately thirty years old."

"That's right."

"Anything else?"

"I can't think of anything, Mr. Speer."

"Think back to when you delivered his sandwich. Just run through it in your mind."

"Okay." Jerry leaned back and shut his eyes. "I got the lemonade and decided to take a roast beef sandwich, too, since Mr. Nichols didn't seem to want to go out to the luau. When I set the tray down on the dresser, there was nothing on it and I remember thinking that was odd. Most people have a water glass, or a package of cigarettes, or something. Mr. Nichols had been in his room for three hours and it looked just like it had when he checked in."

"Good." Mike smiled. "Now, what did Nichols do when you set down the tray."

"Uh . . . nothing. He said all he had were big bills, so he'd catch the tip later. He just stood by the door, waiting for me to leave."

"That was fine, Jerry. Now tell me about the second time."

Jerry nodded. "I went out to the luau and got another sandwich. He opened his door and took the tray. I don't think there was anything unusual . . . oh, wait a second! There was something about his fingers . . ."

All three of them leaned forward, waiting while Jerry tried to remember.

"Oh, yeah." Jerry smiled. "I don't know if it'll help, but Mr. Nichols had purple ink under his thumbnail.

His right thumbnail. I remember wondering how it got there."

"Was he right- or left-handed?" Gina spoke up for the first time.

"Uh . . . left. He signed the register with his left hand. I was working the desk when he checked in."

Amy stared at Gina, whose face had noticeably paled for a second. The poor girl was probably exhausted after performing at the luau and then helping to get the guests resettled. "Why don't you go upstairs, Gina? I'll be up as soon as I can."

"Good idea." Mike finished his coffee and stood up. "You'd better get some rest, too, Jerry. Check into any vacant room. I'll be in touch in the morning."

Mike bent down to kiss Amy as soon as they were alone. He didn't know another woman in the world who'd still be in a good humor if her plans were ruined two nights in a row. "Do you want the bad news or the good news?"

Amy looked up and gave him a small smile. "More bad news?"

"I have to leave again. Hank's waiting for me."

"I figured as much. Go ahead, Mike. Now what's the good news?"

"There's always tomorrow night."

One more kiss and he was gone. Amy turned out the lights in the office and locked the door. She felt very alone.

When Amy got back to the twenty-second floor, the apartment was dark and the door to the guest room was closed. Gina was probably already asleep. Amy went to the kitchen and switched on the light. The open bottle of Dom Pérignon sat on the counter, totally forgotten in the crisis. Amy stared at it for a long moment.

Someone ought to invent a way to put the bubbles back in champagne. It was already flat.

"Just like my plans for tonight. Down the drain." Amy gave a sad little smile and poured the expensive wine in the sink. This was the second bottle of Mike's champagne that had gone to waste.

Katy brushed up against her ankle and Amy leaned down to pick her up. The little calico purred and licked her hand and suddenly Amy felt much better.

Moments later, Amy was under the blankets listening to Katy's contented purr. Everything was fine. She'd get that yellow rose eventually. Just as Mike had said, there was always tomorrow night.

Gina waited until the door to Amy's room had closed before turning on her light again. She had to think.

The moment Jerry had mentioned Mr. Nichols's purple thumbnail, Gina had known exactly who he was describing. Mr. Nichols was Ray Nicolo, a small-time bookie on the west side of Chicago until last year. Ray had always used an indelible pencil and he'd developed the habit of running the point back and forth under his right thumbnail while he'd waited for the result of a race. Today, Ray had a much more important position but he'd hung on to his old habit with the indelible pencil. Ray Nicolo was Vince's right-hand man.

Gina sat down on the edge of her bed and tried to decide what to do. She couldn't risk going to Uncle Claudio without proof but she had to be in Chicago to get it.

Gina opened her suitcase and put it on the bed. She was already forming a plan as she packed. All she had to do was go back home for a few days. Gina knew justice would be swift and sure if Vince were really double-crossing her uncle. It was worth the danger.

Gina snapped the locks on her suitcase and hurried to the bathroom to listen at the connecting door. Everything was quiet; Amy was asleep.

She scribbled a note and left it in the kitchen, propped up against the coffeepot. Amy would find it in the morning when it would be too late to ask questions. Then Gina took the elevator down to the lobby and left a note for Jack. She knew she had to go now, because if she saw him, even one more time, she'd never be able to leave.

Jack shook his head to clear it and rode the escalator down from the second floor of the Midwest airline terminal. He was so tired, he was hallucinating. For a second there, he'd thought he'd seen Gina riding up on the opposite escalator. He hurried to the snack bar and pushed a dollar at the girl behind the counter. "One coffee to go, please."

The girl gave Jack a charming smile as she poured the coffee into a Styrofoam cup and clamped on a lid but Jack didn't even notice. What Gina had told him tonight was enough to make a man mad enough to kill without thinking twice. If he ever found out the name of the guy who'd raped her, he'd make sure he was in no condition to terrorize anyone again.

"Is something wrong, sir?"

Jack looked up as the counter-girl spoke. "No, nothing. Just thinking, that's all."

"I'm glad you're not thinking about me!"

Jack nodded, took the coffee she handed him, and hurried toward the exit. It was time to smoke out

Mike's inside man. Jack figured he was someone in a position of trust, being blackmailed. He'd already checked off most of the vices: drugs, kinky sex, alcoholism. There was only one left.

Jack's cab pulled up in front of what had to be Atlantic City's sleaziest casino, Lucky Lenny's. It was painted day-glow pink and pink neon signs with huge flashing letters claimed the BEST ODDS IN TOWN! Jack tipped the driver and told him to wait. This was Jessie's hangout and Jack's business with him would only take a minute or two.

Lucky Lenny's was packed with what Jack called DG's, Degenerate Gamblers. Most of the people who frequented Lenny's were hard-core night people, the money they earned from odd jobs during the day going straight into Lenny's pocket. It was a small-time operation but Lenny managed to make it pay by running nudie shows upstairs for out-of-towners. Rumor had it you could get anything at Lenny's: whips and chains, young girls, young boys, and, thought Jack as he looked around, every social disease known to man. He found Jessie in an upstairs room, watching two tired hookers mud wrestling.

"Got a job for you, Jessie." Jack tapped his snitch on the shoulder. "Come with me." Jessie looked longingly at one of the wrestlers whose bleached blond hair was streaked with mud, but he followed Jack out to the hallway.

"I want a rundown on any big markers in town. Find out whose they are and whether they've been covered or not. I'll give you ten bucks for every name you can get."

Jessie shrugged elaborately, thin shoulders lifting under the same garish shirt he'd worn in the Dew Drop

Inn. "That's hardly worth it, Jack. People are real sensitive about markers."

"Okay, twenty. Markers over a thousand, got that? Call me as soon as you get something. There'll be a bonus if you find any markers for Speer Palace employees."

Jessie nodded. "Sure, Jack, a thousand-buck bonus if they work at the Palace. I got it. Now can I go? I wanna see that big blonde get mud up her cooze."

The fire trucks had gone and the Speer Palace was still packed with tourists. Now all Jack had to do before bed was call one of his contacts in Chicago. With any luck he might be able to get a couple hours of sleep. A faint smell of smoke in the lobby was the only indication that anything unusual had happened that night. Before he could step into the elevator, a bellboy tapped him on the shoulder. "Here's a message for you, Mr. Humphries. Miss Danello left it at the desk earlier."

Jack tore open the sealed envelope and unfolded the note inside. *Dear Jack,* it said. *I'll be gone for a couple of days. There's a family problem I have to clear up. Love, Gina.* At the bottom of the note there was a line scrawled in the margin. *Thank you for tonight. Someday I'll tell you just how much it meant to me.*

"When did she leave this?" Jack caught the bellboy on his way back to the desk.

"I'm not sure, Mr. Humphries. I came on about ten minutes ago and it was already in your box."

Jack turned and raced for Mike's private elevator. She hadn't mentioned her family before but if there was a problem, he wanted to help. Gina might not realize it but he loved her. He just hoped he could catch her and tell her so.

19

AMY WOKE UP to the sound of the television in the living room and slipped into her robe. Mike was probably trying to relax, watching a John Ford movie. As Amy moved down the hall, she heard a bit of the dialogue. It was Henry Fonda in *My Darling Clementine,* one of her favorite movies. Amy waited until Henry Fonda asked the question. *"Mack, you ever been in love?"*

Then she chimed right in, along with J. Farrell MacDonald, *"No. I been a bartender all my life."*

"Amy!" Mike sat up, startled. "I'm sorry, honey. I didn't mean to wake you."

"I'm glad you did." Amy sat down beside him and grabbed an unopened Nut Goodie. "Do you want a hamburger, Mike? I've got some instant banana cream pudding. Maybe I could sort of pour it over the top for a sauce. We'll call it Banana Nirvana."

Mike laughed and kissed her. It was several minutes before Amy spoke again. "Or I could use one of your Hershey bars. If I tucked about four squares inside the patty, you could have a hamburger *molé.* And if you don't feel like chocolate, I've got . . ."

Mike pulled her into his arms and kissed her again. When they came up for air, Amy went right on talking.

". . . a can of tuna. I could mix it all together for a hamburger *Niçoise.* Or better yet . . ."

Mike clamped his hand over her mouth and put the video tape machine on pause. "Amy, I'm going to tell you a secret but I don't want you to tell another living soul. Do you promise?" Amy managed to nod.

"I'm sick of hamburgers! I started the whole thing as a joke. Chef Sussman got such a kick out of it, I just kept on inventing new ones. Now he expects me to eat hamburgers and you expect me to eat hamburgers and the whole damned staff expects me to eat hamburgers. To tell the truth, I don't care if I ever see another hamburger in my entire life! Now, I'm going to remove my hand if you promise not to ever mention the word *hamburger* again. Promise?"

Amy nodded. If Mike had looked closely he would have seen that her eyes were sparkling.

"There. That's settled." Mike took his hand away. "Now, Amy—"

"Hot dogs!" Amy blurted. "There's chili dogs and cheese dogs, sauerkraut dogs and the kind with the bacon wrapped around them. There's also chicken dogs and turkey dogs and . . ."

Mike groaned and reached out for her. There was obviously only one way to silence Amy. He kissed her hard and long until both of them were trembling. When the kiss was finally over, Amy snuggled up against him and Mike noticed that she didn't say one word. "Gina's sound asleep. Why don't we just open another bottle of champagne . . ."

The doorbell rang. Mike looked as if he couldn't believe his own ears. "Damn! What *is* this?" The doorbell rang again and Mike sighed as he got up to answer it.

"It's called seductus interruptus," Amy muttered to herself as Mike opened the door.

Gina fastened her seatbelt and held her breath as the 747 started down the runway. She'd been lucky to make this flight and she'd even agreed to take the seat next to the window but she'd taken the precaution of pulling down the blind. There was no sense inviting an attack of the willies. She had enough to be nervous about already.

"Is this the first time you've flown, ma'am?" The stewardess tapped Gina on the shoulder.

"Uh . . . no." Gina opened her eyes to see that the No Smoking sign had been turned off and the plane was airborne. She wished that she'd taken up the habit of smoking. People in the movies always smoked when they were nervous.

"Could I bring you a drink? It might help you to relax."

"Oh, yes. That's a good idea." Gina smiled at the friendly stewardess. "Two shots of Tia Maria in a big cup of coffee, please. And make sure it's not decaffeinated."

Ten minutes later the coffee was gone. Gina felt her head spin a little but she could deal with that. The stewardess had been right. Her hands had stopped shaking and she didn't feel nervous anymore. Perhaps courage did come in a bottle.

Gina sighed and leaned back in her seat. She had two hours, enough time to plan out what to tell Uncle Claudio when he asked where she'd been and why she'd run off without a word.

* * *

It was nearly daybreak by the time Jack left. They'd sat up discussing the situation but Gina was gone and there wasn't a damn thing any of them could do about it. Amy had provided Gina's address but the landlord had told Mike she was in Chicago for the summer.

Mike kicked off his shoes. That was better. Then he padded to the bathroom in his stocking feet. Amy had fallen asleep on the couch and Mike had covered her with an afghan. This wasn't the way either one of them had wanted the evening to end.

In a matter of seconds Mike had brushed his teeth and climbed into bed. He turned over on his stomach and closed his eyes but there was a hollow in the mattress he'd never noticed before, centered right under his chest.

The hollow was really bugging him. Mike turned over on his back and stretched out. He tried to decide which was more comfortable, pointing his toes out toward the walls or in, toward each other. He remembered hearing somewhere that the way a person pointed his toes had some deep psychological significance, but for the life of him he couldn't remember which way signified what.

Mike turned over. Sleeping on his side was supposed to be better for his back—he'd read that in some book he'd paged through in the gift shop. Unfortunately, the author of the book didn't explain about arms. The one on top was fine but there was a problem with the arm on the bottom. Either he could keep his arm at his side and cut off his circulation or he could tuck it up, under his pillow. Mike tried both ways but neither of them worked.

Suddenly Mike understood. Thinking about Amy in

the living room, separated from him by only a few feet and a thin wall, would be enough to keep any man awake. He thought about getting up again and carrying her to his bed but that would be positively heartless. Finally, as the sky began to lighten, Mike fell asleep by promising himself that nothing could keep him from Amy tomorrow.

Gina glanced at her watch. It was seven in the morning and she'd spent the past hour sitting in a restaurant at O'Hare, drinking dreadful coffee and waiting for a reasonable hour to call a taxi. She had decided to let Uncle Claudio have his breakfast before she showed up to beg his forgiveness for running away.

"Want a refill, honey?" An overweight waitress stood by Gina's booth, one hand on her ample hip. She wore too much makeup and she was chewing gum. Gina thought she looked like an over-the-hill hooker.

"Uh . . . yes, please."

The waitress leaned over to pour and Gina noticed the green order pad that was tucked into the pocket of her white uniform. The restaurant's slogan was printed in bold type on the top of the order blanks and Gina could read it perfectly through the cheap rayon. SERVING MILLIONS, ALL OVER THE WORLD.

"Too much of this'll rot your stomach, honey." The waitress tapped at the cup with one long fuchsia fingernail. "How about I bring you an order of toast or a glass of milk or something?"

"Well . . . yes. Some toast, I guess." Gina smiled. "You're probably right about the coffee. I've had a lot tonight."

"Six cups here, but who's counting?" The waitress laughed. "Okay, honey. One order of toast coming right up." Gina watched the waitress hurry off to the kitchen, ashamed of herself for being critical of the woman's makeup and fingernails. Ex-hooker or not, she had the proverbial heart of gold.

The toast helped. Gina took her time about eating it, allotting ten minutes to each half-piece, until finally it was eight o'clock. She didn't have much money left but she left a five-dollar tip for the waitress and ten minutes later was in a taxi, heading toward home.

The yellow cab pulled into the driveway at eight-thirty. Gina paid the driver and got out. She could see Uncle Claudio in the kitchen, pouring himself a cup of coffee. He looked just the same and, for a moment, Gina was stunned. Then she realized that she had left less than two days ago. She was the only one who had changed.

"Gina?" Uncle Claudio rushed to the door and hugged her tightly. Gina was amazed to see that he wasn't angry. He just seemed delighted that she was back.

"Uncle Claudio. I'm sorry. I meant to leave you a note but I forgot. A friend of mine called. She was in trouble and she needed me to—"

"No lies!" Claudio's voice was so loud that Gina jumped. "Vince explained. *Coglióne!*"

Gina nodded and kept her silence. Uncle Claudio always mixed in plenty of Italian phrases when he was upset and he forgot that she didn't understand any of them.

"I apologize for my son." Claudio hugged her again. "He's a *cazzomatto* and yet you try to spare me, his father, by making excuses. You're a good girl, Regina, a much better wife than my son deserves."

Gina's mouth opened and snapped closed again. What was Uncle Claudio talking about?

"Come. We'll make all the arrangements. The wedding will be soon. Dixie assures me we can set the date for the end of the month. Vince is very anxious, and so am I." Claudio laughed and draped his arm around her shoulders. "Your wedding day will be the happiest day of my life. Then you'll truly be my daughter, Regina Danello Petrelli."

Gina stood frozen as Claudio kissed her on both cheeks. She scarcely noticed as he grabbed her suitcase and pulled her into the house, calling out for Dixie and Vince. The only thing that registered in Gina's shocked mind were Vince's cold black eyes staring down at her from the top of the stairs. And the hatefully smug expression on his face.

20

IT WAS ELEVEN-THIRTY in the morning, the second day after the fire, and Amy had just finished talking to a group of club members in Texas who had called to cancel their reservations because of the fire. She had done her best to explain that the Speer Palace's sprinkler system had functioned properly and that no one had been hurt but she had gotten nowhere.

Yesterday had been another fiasco as far as the yellow roses were concerned. Both Amy and Mike had been busy dealing with the aftermath of the fire. At six in the evening Mike had suggested a quick dinner in the Dome Room. They hadn't gotten back up to the apartment until nearly eight and by then both of them were exhausted. Mike had fallen asleep on the couch and Amy hadn't had the heart to wake him. She'd gone to bed alone. At least they both had caught up on their sleep.

"Delivery for you, Miss Warner." One of the bellboys knocked on her open door and came in carrying a large box from the flower shop.

"There's a note inside. Fred said to tell you they were ordered by phone . . . a Mr. Roscoe."

"Thank you." Amy reached in her purse to tip the bellboy.

"That's not necessary, Miss Warner. Your smile's all the tip I need."

Amy laughed and glanced at the bellboy's badge. Stan Chassler. He'd go far with a line like that.

Just as soon as the bellboy had left, Amy unwrapped the package. Inside was a single yellow rose and a Speer Palace memo. She laughed as she read it.

To: Miss A. Warner. From: R. Moose. Subject: Rose in Advance. I think you should try love for lunch today, say about noon? Your friend, Roscoe.

Amy didn't even glance at the pile of work on her desk. She just walked out of her office and headed for the elevator. Her secretary looked up from her typing and called after her.

"Miss Warner? Are you going to lunch?"

"Not yet, Joyce. If anyone asks, I'm in an important meeting with Roscoe."

Jessie had called yesterday and promised to get back to him sometime this morning.

"Ring, damn it!" Jack glared at the phone but nothing happened. It sat there solidly, an electronic marvel, defying him. Jack wished that he'd taken up Mike's offer of a secretary. Then she could sit here and wait for the damned thing to ring.

Jack knew his irritation would disappear in a hurry if she walked through the door, but none of his contacts had even heard of Gina Danello. It was a hell of a mess.

Jack sat down in his chair and pulled open his center desk drawer. Inside was a black felt-tip pen and a Speer Palace memo pad. He took them out and drew a large tic-tac-toe grid. His right hand would be *X* and his left hand would be *O*. After a ten to nine victory for the left, Jack quit. There had to be something else he could do while he was waiting for Jessie's call to come in. Idly, he tore off the top sheet of paper and folded it into a paper airplane. Then he flew it across the room. Not bad. Maybe with a little different wing design . . .

Twenty minutes later Jack had perfected his craft. It looked damned good and it flew even better than it looked. Perhaps he should have gone into aeronautical design. At least then he wouldn't have to sit around waiting for the phone to . . .

Jack grabbed the phone before the first ring was completed. "This is Jack Humphries."

He listened for a moment and frowned. "Right, Jessie. Do I bring the bonus?"

There was a pause while Jack gripped the receiver tightly. "You're sure about that?"

The voice on the other end of the line said something that made Jack sit up straight. "Okay, Jessie. Stay put. I'll be right there."

"Alone, at last!" Mike popped the cork on another bottle of champagne and poured Amy a glass. They were sitting on the patio in matching chaise longues, and although the sun was at a midpoint in the sky, a cooling sea breeze rustled the leaves on the potted trees. Both of them knew they should be working and that made this stolen interlude even more delicious. It felt almost like playing hookey from school.

"You're sure no one's going to come looking for you?" Amy accepted the glass Mike offered.

"Flip's in a meeting with the food servers' union and Hank's briefing his men on the new security schedule. We're safe, Amy. No telephone, I unplugged it. No doorbell. Everyone with my elevator code's tied up for the afternoon."

"Good!" Amy took a sip of champagne and wiggled out of her dress. Now she was glad she'd worn her very best lingerie. The expression on Mike's face was worth every penny of the ridiculous price she'd paid. The slip was the next thing to go. Mike caught his breath as Amy stood there in the sunlight, in nothing but a wisp of pale peach lace at her breasts and her thighs. The lace was nearly transparent and the strong sunlight made it damned near invisible. Mike groaned as he crossed the space that separated them and took her in his arms. At last. Just as he was about to pull her down on the soft, thick grass, the doorbell rang.

Jack stood outside the door, shifting from foot to foot. What was taking him so long?

At last the door jerked open and Jack stepped back as he caught the expression on Mike's face. "Oh, hey! I'm sorry, Mike. I didn't mean to interrupt anything." Jack knew he'd better make his explanation in a hurry. "Jessie's got information about your inside man. He couldn't get a name but he's got plenty of dates and places."

Mike sighed deeply. "Okay, Jack. Come in and wait in the living room. I'll be with you in just a minute."

By the time Mike got out on the patio, Amy was dressed again. "Uh . . . Amy? I don't know how to say this but . . ."

"But there's always tonight." Amy gave him a half-hearted grin. "Go ahead, Mike. It wouldn't have worked out anyway. I think God's trying to protect my virtue."

Mike laughed but he couldn't help but wonder if she had a point. It *did* seem like some kind of cosmic interference. He'd have to figure out some way to fool the fates, right after his talk with Jack.

Flip was shaking as he pulled the Datsun up next to the warehouse. It was a combination of fear and exhilaration. He was going to take a stand. Even though he hated cigars, Flip unwrapped the five-dollar Havana he'd bought at the hotel smokeshop and jammed it in his mouth. Of course it was a prop, but it made him feel almost as tough as Edward G. Robinson.

The dust-colored sedan rolled up and parked a distance away. Flip deliberately ignored it. The driver could come to him for a change. Everything was different now. It took a full five minutes but finally the sedan's powerful engine roared into life and the car screeched up beside his Datsun. Flip raised his eyebrows and looked straight into the driver's eyes. The man seemed wary and that made Flip feel good.

"Hand it over, asshole." The driver stuck his hand out the window.

Flip frowned in what he hoped was a tough manner. "Haven't got it, asshole."

The man blinked once. Then he smiled his terrible smile. "Mr. Petrelli's not going to like that."

"Good." Flip smiled back. The longer he held the smile, the better he felt. "Tell Vince he'd better lay off the Speer Palace if he knows what's good for him."

The driver turned livid and his eyes bored into Flip's but Flip didn't give an inch. It seemed like hours but finally the man slammed the car into gear and drove away.

Flip laughed out loud as the sedan roared off, scattering gravel and dirt. The Datsun started on the first try and Flip pulled out into traffic. He'd told Vince

Petrelli's man to fuck off and he was still alive. Maybe the Mafia wasn't all it was cracked up to be in the movies. Flip reached for the soundtrack of *The Godfather* and put it in the tapedeck. His hands tightened on the wheel as it started to play. The scene in the tollbooth flashed through his mind and it occurred to Flip that maybe he was pushing his luck. He settled for *Simon and Garfunkel's Greatest Hits* instead.

Vince sat in his high-rise apartment, waiting for the news. In less than an hour he'd have access to Mike Speer's penthouse and the fun would start. Speer would trot right down to R. D. Pierce's office and sign the Palace over nice and legal the moment he found out that his blonde had been nabbed from right under his fucking nose. Now Vince was glad he hadn't given the order to hit her that night at the dump.

Everything was turning out even better than Vince had expected. Gina was back and those fucking wedding plans would keep his father and mother occupied for weeks.

Vince laughed out loud as he thought of the wedding. It was going to be a real Guinea affair. Everyone was invited, even Claudio's godson. Naturally, Vince had approved the guest list.

On the way from the church to the reception, Papa and Mama would have a little accident on the expressway. If he could figure out some way to get the bride in the car with them, better yet. No one would suspect the grieving bridegroom and it would be one hell of a wedding present.

The phone rang and Vince's face hardened as he listened to his man in New Jersey. The little prick had screwed up but Vince's man was resourceful. He'd found an air-conditioning vent that was large enough for a man to crawl through. There would be no problem getting into Speer's penthouse when the time was right.

"Take care of it for me, Mario." Vince leaned back on his chair and crossed his legs. "Give me a call when it's over. I'll leave the answering machine on. Oh, yeah. When you do that job tonight? It wouldn't hurt if a couple of guests just happened to get in the way."

Amy carried their champagne glasses into the living room and filled a third glass for Jack. "You've got to help us drink this, Jack. I'm getting tired of pouring stale champagne down the drain."

Jack took the glass and his naturally ruddy complexion turned even redder. "I apologize, Amy. I tried to call first but Alice couldn't get through. I never would have interrupted but . . . well . . . this is really important."

"It's all right, Jack." Mike took their friend off the hook. "Amy and I've learned to take interruptions in stride."

Amy perched on the edge of Mike's chair. Jack had interrupted the best striptease of her life but she managed a smile anyway. "Mike said you had some information about the inside man?"

"Right. My contact, Jessie, couldn't get a name but I've got plenty of hints. We know he works at the Speer Palace and you handle all the personnel records, Amy. Maybe something will ring a bell."

Jack glanced down at the notes he'd made. "I'll start with the most recent thing I have. Our man played poker at Benny's Bankroll three nights ago. He lost a thousand but he covered it. Jessie brought me one of the guys who sat in on the game but he couldn't give me much of a description. Medium height, medium build, blondish hair. He remembers our man was wearing a white cowboy shirt with a red rose embroidered over the pocket but that's about it."

Amy nodded. The description was too general to help much and that particular style of cowboy shirt was popular. She'd given Flip one just like it for Christmas last year.

"Jessie got a little more from Lucky Lenny's. Our man was there on the first of the month. He lost three thousand, covered half, and gave Lenny a diamond pinky ring to hold, promising to pay off the rest the next day. Jessie got a look at the ring because Lenny wore it awhile before he put it in the safe. It had a circle of diamonds around a gold nugget."

Amy's heart pounded so hard she was afraid Mike and Jack could hear it. Flip had a ring like that but he never wore it in the casino because he said it was too flashy. She tried to remember the date Flip had borrowed fifteen hundred dollars from her. It was the day after she paid her August rent, the second. When Jack described a gold rabbit's foot the man carried, Amy knew for certain. She had designed that charm herself and given it to Flip for his birthday.

"There's more, but it's heresay. Our man's run up some big markers in Reno but he's got unlimited credit because Petrelli bought them up. The same in Tahoe and Vegas. Jessie tried to get a name but all anyone would tell him was that our man has an important position at the Speer Palace. No one wants to snitch on a guy who works for the Petrellis."

"Amy . . . are you all right?" Both men looked at Amy in alarm as her face turned pale.

Swallowing hard, Amy opened her mouth but no

words came out. How could she tell the man she loved that her own brother was a traitor?

Amy made an excuse about checking personnel records and promised to be back in a few minutes. The least she owed Flip was a personal confrontation.

"Amy?" Flip looked pleased to see her until he got a good look at her face. "What's wrong?"

Amy walked into the room and closed the door. "Why did you do it, Flip? Mike's always been your best friend!"

Flip had been standing when Amy barged into the office but now he sank down into his chair. "Does Mike know?"

"Not yet, but if you don't go up and tell him yourself, I will. Why, Flip? Just tell me why!"

The sight of his sister's contorted face was almost more than Flip could bear. He blurted out the whole shameful story, the way he'd gotten into trouble in Nevada and how a man who he'd thought was a buddy had bailed him out. How he'd sworn to stop gambling when he went to work for Mike and how he'd failed. And the favors his buddy had demanded, little ones at first, ones that couldn't possibly hurt anyone, then bigger ones until by the time he'd discovered what the Petrellis really wanted it had been too late. Between their threats and his weakness they had owned him.

They were both crying when Flip had finished. Amy had come in fueled with shame and anger but now she felt nothing but sadness. "You've got to tell Mike." Amy put her arm around her brother. Now she was the strong one.

"I know."

They rode up in the elevator together, holding hands.

Amy wasn't sure what to expect. Mike had a right to hate Flip for what he'd done but she hoped he'd eventually understand. Flip was a traitor and he'd done an awful thing but he desperately needed their help.

Jack and Mike were still sitting on the couch. Amy hovered anxiously by her brother as the story came out.

"You?!" Mike looked incredulous at first, but then his eyes hardened into a white rage. "I trusted you!"

"I know you did." Flip's hands were shaking but somehow he found the courage to meet Mike's accusing eyes, empty of any trace of their years of friendship. Mike faced him like a prosecuting attorney. "I want dates, times, names. Take it down, Jack. And if I find that you've held out on me, I'll kill you."

Amy reached out for Mike's shoulder but he shrugged her off. She knew better than to follow him out of the room. She'd never seen Mike this angry before.

Mike strode across the patio and banged his fist into the side of one of the redwood tubs. The whole tree shuddered with his blow. He hit it again, so hard that the wood splintered. He'd wanted to smash the little bastard at first but he couldn't in front of Amy.

There was a faucet near the Jacuzzi and Mike turned it on full blast, splashing it up against his face. The ice cold water was a shock and, after a minute, he shook his head and wiped his face on a towel. That was better. Now he had to calm down enough to think.

For twenty minutes Amy sat on the edge of the couch listening to Flip and Jack, twisting her hands together anxiously. When she heard the patio door open it was all she could do not to jump up and beg Mike to spare her brother.

"Have you got it, Jack?" Mike stood in the doorway, his face impassive. Jack nodded.

"All right, Flip, think hard. Did your contact ever mention Claudio Petrelli's name?"

"No. It was always Mr. Petrelli. Or Vince."

"All right, Flip. I want you to stick to Amy tonight like glue. Have dinner at the Dome Room as if nothing happened. Jack and I have things to do. If anyone asks for us, tell them we're somewhere on the floor. Got it?"

"Uh . . . yes!" Flip was stunned. He'd expected the worst.

"Tomorrow I'll get you some help for your gambling problem. It's a disease, and just like alcoholism, you can beat it." Mike's eyes softened as he looked at his childhood friend. "I don't understand why you didn't tell me. I would have been mad at first, but I've always bailed you out. All you had to do was remember who taught you to handle that punching bag at Thorton."

"My contact in Chicago came through." Jack flopped down in a chair in front of Mike's desk. "Vince Petrelli lives in a high-rise on Lake Shore Drive. He's going to be gone tonight, some kind of family party, and I figure I can get in and out before he gets back."

"What's the risk factor, Jack?"

Jack shrugged. "I've cracked a couple of these kind of security buildings before. It should be a piece of cake."

Mike nodded and picked up the phone. "Judy? Get me the travel agency, please."

Jack sat back and relaxed as Mike talked to the travel agent, glad Mike had bought his line. If Mike knew how dangerous tonight would really be, he might have called off the whole thing.

"Right. First class, round trip. For two."

It took a second for Mike's words to register and then Jack sat bolt upright. "Hey! We don't need two tickets."

"Sure we do. One for you and one for me."

Mike hung up the phone and grinned at Jack's shocked face. "What are you so upset about? You told me it was a piece of cake."

21

GINA SLIPPED THE heavy cream-colored silk dress over her head and fastened it at the waist. She still felt embarrassed over what it had cost Uncle Claudio. Gina didn't care one way or the other about the designer label but Dixie had been insistent on something expensive and utterly tasteful for the party tonight.

Things were rolling along much too fast to suit Gina. She had to find that proof soon, before she found herself kneeling at the altar with that bastard. Their engagement was being announced tonight, at Claudio and Dixie's fortieth anniversary party. Dixie had been planning the party for months now, and all the right people would be there. Both Dixie and Claudio felt there was no reason to delay the good news.

The house was all decked out for the occasion. Dixie had hired a maid service and the house had been cleaned from top to bottom. The florist had come in this morning and arranged flowers in every room. After the gift-opening ceremony, there would be a huge outdoor buffet under the canopy that the caterers had set up in the parklike backyard. Then, after everyone had eaten, Claudio would announce Vince's engagement.

Gina looked out the window to see that cars were

already arriving. Dixie had invited more than three hundred guests and it would be easy to slip away without being noticed. The orchestra was tuning up in the garden. Gina could hear faint strains of something that sounded like Henry Mancini. She ran a quick comb through her hair and stepped back to look in the mirror.

"Are you ready, Gina dear?" Dixie knocked on her door sharply and Gina hurried to open it. Dixie had been calling her "Gina dear" ever since she had agreed to marry Vince. Dixie was dressed in a Bill Blass original of shimmering turquoise satin that draped low over the bodice ending in a floor-length sheath.

"Good heavens, that'll never do." Dixie frowned as she saw Gina. "Smile, Gina, smile! This should be the happiest night of your life."

Gina fixed her face in a smile that managed to pass Dixie's scrutiny.

"That's much better, Gina dear. You look positively radiant. Come along now, our guests are arriving." As Gina followed Dixie down the stairs, her smile grew wider . . . with the anticipation of her revenge.

The Petrellis' anniversary party was in full swing and Dixie had just begun the gift-opening.

"Oh, that's gorgeous! Thank you, Angelina. Isn't this lovely, Claudio?"

Claudio nodded. He was smiling politely but Gina noticed that he looked bored. This was only the third gift to be unwrapped and that meant there were at least a hundred and fifty to go. Gina edged her way back through the crowd surrounding the anniversary couple. She breathed a sigh of relief when she made it to the stairs. A moment later she was in her room, changing to a less conspicuous outfit.

As Gina started down the stairs, she heard Vince on the phone in the alcove below. She stopped, intending to go back upstairs and use the outside stairway, but something furtive in Vince's voice alerted her. "Listen, Frank. I'm going to be tied up longer than I thought and there's a piece coming over in an hour or so. Her name's Suzanne. Let her in and tell her to go up and wait for me."

Frank must have said something funny because Vince laughed. Gina didn't wait around to hear the rest of his conversation. She raced to the outside staircase and went straight to the garage.

"You're leaving the party, Miss Danello?" Uncle Claudio's man at the gate was shocked.

"Just for a couple of minutes, Sal. The store delivered the wrong present and I've got to pick up the right one before they finish opening the gifts."

Sal nodded and waved her through. He understood the importance of having the right gift for the don's anniversary. It was a sign of respect.

The drive to Vince's apartment took only ten minutes. Gina drove past the expensive brick building and parked around the corner. Then she walked around the block and came in through the front entrance.

"I'm supposed to meet Mr. Petrelli."

The man at the desk grinned knowingly. "Name, please?"

"Suzanne."

"Mr. Petrelli called. He's gonna be a little late but he said you should go up and wait for him. Fifth floor. I'll tell them to let you in."

Gina made it all the way to the elevator before the guard called her name.

"Wait a second. Mr. Petrelli said you were a redhead."

Gina thought fast. When she turned around she had a smile on her face. "That was last week. Next week I'll be a blonde."

The guard laughed and picked up the phone again. Gina was shaking as she got into the elevator. She just hoped none of Vince's men had ever seen Suzanne before. The guards let her in, almost too easily. Gina took a quick look through the apartment. She was alone. With any luck she could find the evidence and be out of here in less than five minutes.

The apartment covered the whole floor, and one of the four bedrooms had been equipped as an office. Gina noticed that the red light on Vince's answering machine was blinking and the counter was on the number one. She turned down the volume to a barely audible level and replayed his message.

"This is Ray. I checked on the car for you. It goes in for servicing next week and the mechanic that usually works on it isn't going to make it to the garage that morning. We lucked out. The other guys don't know shit about working on that Mercedes so I got my own man in there today. He'll put in a box with a time switch. One of the valet parkers at St. Steven's will throw it when he brings the car up front."

For a long moment Gina just stared at the machine, stunned. Then she switched off the recorder and took out the tape. Uncle Claudio had a Mercedes. And St. Steven's was the church where her wedding was scheduled.

She was at the door before she remembered the

guards outside. They'd be sure to search her. She had to find another way out. Gina slid open the patio door. It was the fifth floor and it took all the courage she possessed to grip the railing and look over the side. There was a balcony below her. If she hung from her hands, it would be only about a three foot drop to the floor below. She knew she had the coordination, but she doubted that she could force herself to climb over the railing.

Another quick trip through the apartment convinced Gina that the balcony was the only way out. What would Jack do in a situation like this? Gina tried to think. The first thing would be to make sure that Uncle Claudio got the tape, even if something went wrong.

Gina wrote her uncle's name and address on the tape and stuffed it inside her bra, securing it with some adhesive strips from Vince's medicine chest. The guards had no reason to doubt her identity and people would gather around if she fell. There would be no opportunity to search her and there was a good chance the tape would get to Uncle Claudio, eventually. Now what would Jack do next?

The moment Gina thought of it, she started her search. Jack would look for a climbing rope. Gina searched frantically for a full five minutes and finally she found some strong cord in a kitchen drawer. It would have to do. Now she was glad she'd spent the first day in that awful rock climbing class, before her transfer to Hawaiian dancing had come through. At least she'd learned something about knots.

Gina cut off a length of cord and tied it around her body in a half sling. If the cord held, it would catch her as she dropped over the rail.

The balcony door was still open and Gina stepped

out. She was shaking so hard, she could barely tie the cord to the rail. She tried to remember exactly how the instructor had done it in the Fairview classroom. Gina knew that if she'd used the proper knot, she'd be able to pull the cord down after her when she landed safely on the balcony below. Of course if the knot was wrong . . .

Gina deliberately pushed that possibility out of her mind. Her heart was pounding and she faltered as she straddled the railing. She wouldn't think. She'd just pretend that Jack was waiting below, to take her into his arms. The wind whipped through Gina's hair as she gripped the rope, shut her eyes, and let herself fall.

Karen Ferguson was watching *Dallas* when her son Jimmy screamed. She ran into the bedroom and switched on the light. Jimmy was sitting up in bed, staring at the window.

"What's the matter, honey?" Karen went over to take the five-year-old in her arms.

"A face, Mommy! There was a face outside my window!"

"You were dreaming, sweetheart." Karen wiped his face and kissed him. "We're on the fourth floor, Jimmy. Nobody's that tall. Go back to sleep, honey. It was just a bad dream, that's all." Karen held the boy until he relaxed. Then she tucked him in, gave him another kiss, and waited until he went back to sleep.

The rope tightened painfully under her arms. Gina gasped and her eyes flew open. The fourth floor balcony was directly in front of her. All she had to do was swing her feet forward, hook them around the rail and she'd be safe. A moment later she was climbing over the railing onto the patio. Gina grabbed the short end of the rope and pulled sharply. She didn't realize she'd been holding her breath until the rope tumbled down in her hand, releasing exactly the way the rock climbing instructor had said it would.

The second time, it was easier. Gina still had to force herself over the rail but she managed to keep her eyes open on the way down. Now she was on the third floor balcony. Only two to go. Another ten minutes and she was down. Gina went weak with relief when her feet touched the grass. She yanked on the rope to release it and stuffed it into her pocket. Then she turned to look back up at the fifth floor balcony.

Her heart pounded hard in her chest when she saw the distance she'd climbed. Gina looked back at the ground until her dizziness passed, and gave a shaky smile. She might just have made it through that rock climbing class, after all.

22

AMY FINISHED THE last of her wine and stood up. Dinner at the Dome Room had been excellent, as usual, but neither she nor Flip had been able to do justice to Chef Sussman's swordfish steak with caviar sauce.

Flip pushed the button for the elevator. "I have to stop by my room to pick up some things. You'll have to come along, Amy, I promised Mike I wouldn't leave you alone."

Amy nodded. Even though Flip had tried his best to cheer her up during dinner, she was still worried. Mike had called to say he was flying to Chicago with Jack, and twice mentioned that it was just a routine business trip. But Amy knew the Petrellis lived in Chicago.

The elevator stopped on Flip's floor and Amy spotted Jake working at the end of the corridor. "Hi, Jake."

"Hello, Miss Warner. Oh, Mr. Warner? There were a couple of guys knocking on your door a while back. They said they'd be around again."

"Okay, Jake. Thanks for telling me."

Jake turned back to his Gucci loafers just as soon as they'd gone inside. He thought Mr. Warner looked better than he had in a long time. Jake had tried to analyze what it was about Mr. Warner that made him feel sad. There had been a defeated look in his eyes like a condemned man. Tonight, that look was gone.

The elevator bell rang, just as Jake finished the last pair of shoes. Perfect timing. He had to run down to the lobby to get some more brown polish before he started in on the next floor.

Jake stuffed his brushes and polish in his box and hefted it to his shoulder. The box weighed about seventy pounds when it was full and Jake restocked it every night. Mr. Speer ordered the very best supplies for him. He'd built the box himself, when he started out in the business over forty years ago, from scraps he'd found at an abandoned lumber yard. Just last week one of the guests had told him the wood was mahogany and offered to buy it for a hundred dollars. Jake had refused, politely, of course. His grandson would inherit this box someday. Even if he didn't go into the business, it would bring him luck.

The elevator doors opened and the two men who'd been knocking on Mr. Warner's door got out. Jake didn't notice their shoes until the elevator doors started to close. "Jesus, God in Heaven!"

Jake whispered the words as he hit the stop button. There wasn't time to go for help. The big man was knocking on the door now and the other one was reaching into his jacket, pulling out a gun. Jake didn't take time to consider the consequences. He just hollered as loud as he could.

"Watch out, Mr. Warner! They're gonna kill you!"

Jake yelled and Mr. Warner's door slammed closed, a scant instant before the gun went off. The big man whirled and fired a shot through the closing elevator doors. Jake heard his mahogany box splinter and the impact slammed him up against the control panel. The doors slid closed and the elevator began to descend.

There was a burning pain in his chest. Jake tried to hold himself up, but he slid down the glass mirror on the wall, crumpling to the floor. He looked down at his chest and saw a red stain spreading out over his best uniform jacket.

The elevator doors opened. There were people waiting to get on. One woman screamed loudly. Jake looked up and tried to tell her that he wasn't hurt as bad as it looked but his voice didn't work right and he couldn't seem to move. Then everything turned very black.

Karen Ferguson frowned as the phone rang. Between Jimmy's nightmare and the phone, she was missing most of tonight's episode of *Dallas.*

"Mrs. Ferguson? Karen Ferguson?"

"Yes?"

"This is Freddy Fontanna, the top banana on station KTZ. Are you listening to our program tonight?"

"Uh . . . no." Karen laughed a little. "I'm watching *Dallas.*"

"Then this is your lucky night, Karen. We'll all find out why in just a minute. But first, let me tell you about our latest contest. You're still with me, aren't you, Karen?"

"Yes, I'm still here."

"Your name, Karen, was drawn out of a revolving drum by our own, Miss Chicago. And if you can answer one simple question, you'll win a super-dooper sampler of the best pizza in the Windy City. Are you ready for the KTZ question?"

"Uh . . . yes."

"Name the actor who plays J.R. on *Dallas.*"

Jack stepped out of the phone booth and got back into the waiting taxi.

"Take us to the nearest pizza place, and step on it. You'll get a five-buck tip if you don't waste time." The cabbie pulled out into traffic with a screech and Jack laughed as Mike shot him a surprised look.

"We've got a couple of deliveries to make . . . on Lake Shore Drive."

Within ten minutes Jack and Mike were back in the taxi, each holding a take-out box. Jack gave the address of Vince's apartment and sat back to enjoy the ride. The cabbie was driving like a New Yorker and it made him feel right at home.

"Just let us off here." Jack tapped the cab driver on the shoulder and motioned for him to pull up at the end of the block. The two men waited for the driver to pull away and then they walked up to the entrance.

"Delivery for Mrs. Karen Ferguson." Jack grinned at the man behind the desk.

"Right. She called down. It's the fourth floor. Take that elevator over there."

Mike waited in the hallway while Jack made the delivery. Then they got into the elevator again and rode up to the fifth floor.

"Pizza delivery." Mike stepped up to the guard that stood in front of Vince's door.

"We didn't order a pizza."

"You're kidding!" Mike shook his head. "This is the second one tonight. Mr. Roger Overland called it in. I've got the address right here . . . see?"

The second guard came over to look at the ticket taped on the box. "That's the right address but the wrong name. Somebody's fucked up."

"It'll just get cold on the ride back. Here, you can have it."

Mike shoved the box into the second guard's arms just as Jack jumped the first one. In a matter of seconds both guards were trussed up like Christmas turkeys.

"Okay . . . let's get the stuff and get out!"

Jack used the guard's key to unlock the door and they dragged the two men inside. A quick survey of the apartment led them to Vince's safe in the office.

"Okay . . . you go check on those guards. I'll have this open in just a second."

Mike didn't ask any questions. Jack was the expert on things like safecracking. He checked the guards and was just starting back to the office when he heard a muffled explosion.

When Mike rushed back into the office, he saw Jack coming out of a crouch behind the desk. There was a jagged hole in the side of the safe.

"Jesus, Jack! I didn't know you were going to blow it."

"There wasn't time to try to crack it." Jack went over to examine the safe. "This plastique is great stuff."

"You've used it a lot?"

"Nope. Tonight was the first time. Come on, Mike, let's grab these papers and get out of here. Somebody's going to report that explosion."

Karen Ferguson picked up the phone to call the desk. The noise she'd heard was probably just a car backfiring but she wanted to make sure. She always got nervous when Chuck was out of town and she was alone with Jimmy for the night.

Just then Jimmy screamed again. Karen hung up the phone and ran to the bedroom. She found her son sitting up in bed again, his pajamas drenched with sweat.

"Mommy, two faces this time! I counted them! There were two faces at the window, honest!"

"Oh, Jimmy!" Karen hugged him tightly. The poor darling. He must have had the same nightmare again.

"Let's pull the drapes, sweetheart. Maybe that'll keep you from having those bad dreams." Karen walked to the window and pulled the drapes. When she attempted to tuck Jimmy under the covers again, he threw his arms around her neck and held on tight.

"Mommy? I'm scared!"

"Okay, honey." Karen gave in to the inevitable. "You can stay up with me for a while. I've even got a surprise in the living room."

Jimmy grinned as he crawled out of bed and followed his mother. He seemed to forget all about his scare as Karen handed him a big piece of the super-dooper sampler. Pizza was a real treat for Jimmy. She never gave him spicy food at night because Chuck was sure it caused nightmares.

Karen smiled as Jimmy wolfed down his pizza and settled right down with his head on her lap. His eyes closed and in a matter of minutes, he was asleep. She moved him to the end of the couch and covered him with an afghan. Then she switched the television to the ABC movie of the week. It was one she'd missed in the theaters, *Nine to Five.*

There were four pieces of pizza left. Karen took one

and leaned back against the cushions to watch the movie. She became so engrossed in trying to figure out if Dolly Parton was real or silicone that she forgot all about calling the desk.

Mike was still puffing hard as they arrived at a phone booth, four blocks away. Just as soon as he'd caught his breath, he turned to Jack accusingly. "You didn't tell me we'd have to climb down four balconies."

"You didn't ask. Come on, Mike. Call a taxi so we can crash Claudio's party. We've got all the proof we need."

"We've got nothing."

Jack turned to look at Mike in surprise. "What do you mean? There's stock certificates in Speer International with Vince Petrelli's name on them. There's an account of the money he paid to Cardinelli to delay the building permits and to hijack that shipment of chips. There's a report of the elevator mugging. There's even a copy of a note telling Cardinelli to kidnap Amy!"

"Just like I said, Jack. We've got nothing."

"Jesus Christ, Mike! What do you mean?"

"I can't use any of it. It's a matter of honor, Jack. If I used these papers tonight, Claudio would lose face. He'll never admit it, but Greeks and Italians are alike in a lot of ways. This is one time you have to shut up and trust me."

"Then why did we break in and grab that stuff? I don't understand!"

"I needed to find out for sure, and I did. Do you have a book of matches?"

Jack winced but he pulled a book of matches out of his pocket and handed it to Mike. There was a sick expression on his face as he watched Mike burn the papers but he didn't say a word. "Now I'll call that taxi."

"Okay." Jack sighed. "I sure hope you know what you're doing."

Mike waited until they were halfway to Claudio's house before he spoke again. "Have you figured out a way to crash Claudio's party, yet?"

"Not really. That one's up to you. I've done all the work so far, except for that little bonfire in the phone booth."

Mike laughed. Jack had accepted his action even though he didn't understand it. That was true friendship. He pulled an envelope out of his pocket and handed it over. "This came in yesterday's mail. We don't have to crash. It's an invitation from Claudio."

Jack leaned back against the seat and nodded. "I knew there was some reason I talked you into coming along."

Claudio Petrelli sat in his office, listening to the tape again. He had sent Gina away after she had answered his questions. Gina was a good girl. She had come to him with tears in her eyes because she had no choice but to hurt him.

His intercom buzzed and Claudio reached out to answer it. Mike Speer and his friend had arrived. "Bring them to me, Sal."

Claudio leaned back in his chair and sipped the anisette that Gina had poured for him before she had left. It had been a simple matter to confirm what Gina had said. Claudio had already received word that Vince was behind Mike's troubles at the Speer Palace. It was possible to be more lenient with his wife, she would suffer enough when this night was over, but his son had disgraced the family name. There was only one action a man of honor could take.

"Godfather."

Claudio looked up as Mike entered the room. He had been prepared to overlook Mike's ignorance of the customs but Mike startled him by kissing his hand. "First I come to pay my respects, and then to congratulate you on your anniversary. I'd like you to meet my friend, Jack Humphries. Jack, this is my godfather, Claudio Petrelli."

Claudio studied this friend of Mike's as he shook his hand. Red hair, powerfully built, probably Irish. Claudio had no quarrel with the Irish. An Irish family had shared food with him long ago, when he and Nicholas had first arrived in this country. So this was the man Gina loved. Perhaps he might approve of the match.

"I brought you a small gift, in honor of your anniversary." Mike handed Claudio an envelope.

Claudio opened it with steady hands, even though his heart was filled with dread. He expected to find the contents of Vince's safe. He knew Mike and his friend had broken into the apartment on Lake Shore Drive.

"Ten shares of the Speer Palace?" Claudio looked down at the paper in shock. Mike knew that Vince had tried to sabotage his business. Why was he doing this?

"As a favor to me, I hope you'll take an active part in advising me, Godfather. I would like to see my gift grow in value over the years."

Claudio looked at Mike in astonishment. Then he smiled as he understood. By presenting these shares in the Speer Palace, Mike was asking him to take an active interest in the business. It was a way for Claudio to discover the truth on his own. It was a courageous thing to do. His sources had told him that Mike had barely enough capital to hold on for another month.

"Thank you." There were tears in Claudio's eyes and he stood to kiss Mike on both cheeks. His godson was giving him a way to save face. There was only one explanation: Claudio was positive that Michael Spiros, the Greek, had some long-forgotten Italian relatives.

"Now there is a favor I must ask of you, Michael."

"Anything, Godfather."

"I ask you to protect my most priceless possession. I feel sure that your friend will help you. Do you agree?"

"Yes, Godfather."

Claudio smiled as he pressed the intercom. "Tell my niece to come in. She's to go with these two men and stay until I send for her."

Both Mike and his friend swallowed hard when Gina walked in. To their credit they said nothing, even though the Irishman's face betrayed him. Claudio was pleased; Gina would be in good hands until this was over. It was plain to see that the Irishman loved her.

After they had left, Claudio picked up his glass of anisette and drained it. Then he reached for the telephone with a steady hand. It took only one call to make the arrangements. There was *protocòllo* for a situation such as this. In time he might be able to forget, but he would never forgive.

Vince Petrelli gunned the motor and waited impatiently for Ray to get into the passenger seat of the Jaguar. He couldn't believe his hair-brained mother forgetting to pick up the anniversary cake and the old man had ordered him to drive to the bakery to get it.

"It's at The House of Cakes, on Thirtieth and

Jefferson." Ray crumpled up the directions Claudio had given him and stuffed them in his pocket. "Your father said the fastest way to get there is to cut through the hills. There shouldn't be any traffic this time of night."

"Yeah, Ray. I know how to get there."

"Your father also said to tell you *Mene, mene, tekel, upharsin.*"

"Christ! The old man's got a stupid wop saying for everything!"

"That's not like any Italian I ever heard."

"Sure, it's pig latin!" Vince put the car in gear and roared down the driveway. He took the curves so fast the tires squealed, but the powerful car hugged the road and in less than five minutes they were cutting through the hills. New construction was booming in this area but the huge housing developments were far from completed.

"Open the glovebox, Ray. We've got time for a quick snort before we hit traffic again."

The light came on in the compartment as Ray passed the vial to Vince. "Hey, Vince. You forgot to take in your old man's present."

"What present?" Vince glanced over at the gift-wrapped box and frowned. He'd just remembered what his father's saying meant. It was from the Bible and Claudio had used it when Vince was a little boy, as a prelude to a spanking. *Mene, mene tekel upharsin. You have been weighed on the scales and found wanting.*

Vince hit the brakes, hard. "Toss out that package, Ray! The old man's set us up!"

Ray was reaching for the window when the box exploded. A glowing comet of fiery metal, the car hurtled through the guard rail into a manmade pond a hundred and fifty feet below the crest of the hill. It hit nose first, plowing through the stagnant water until its momentum slowed, then slowly sinking beneath the algae-covered surface with a great shower of sparks and a cloud of hissing steam. For several minutes bubbles broke the surface of the water and then the night was silent again.

23

THE CHAMPAGNE SAT in a silver ice bucket on the table, next to the bed. Two glasses, partially empty, rested beside it. Amy was wrapped in Mike's arms appropriately dressed in nothing at all.

"You don't know how long I've waited for this!" Mike's voice was shaking a little.

"Oh, yes I do."

"Shhh, don't say anything. You might jinx us."

"It's all right, Mike. Flip's at the hospital, waiting to bring Jake home. Do you realize that shoeshine box saved his life?"

Mike nodded.

"And Hank called me about an hour ago. He's going home early for a change. That leaves Jack and he's with Gina. Nobody else has this number."

"Right." Mike held her tightly and stroked her hair. "Now, don't you think it's about time we stopped talking and . . ."

The telephone rang loudly and both of them froze. It rang again and Mike reached out to answer it. Alice's sexy voice came on the line. "I heard you were back and I thought I'd better call right away. I'm not interrupting anything, am I?"

"Nothing that hasn't been interrupted before."

There was a moment of silence as Alice digested Mike's comment.

"Well . . . Amy told me to put through anyone who heard that Crunch-Bird joke. I've got five people on hold and they all want to tell it. Hang on a second and I'll arrange a conference call."

Mike covered the mouthpiece with his hand. "Alice has five people who heard the Crunch-Bird joke. She's putting them all on at once."

Amy wanted to laugh but she managed to look contrite. "I'm sorry, Mike. It's my fault. I told Alice to ring here if she found anybody who'd heard that stupid joke."

"All set, Mr. Speer. I've got Fred from the flower shop, Bobby Marrin from the casino, Stan Chassler, your newest bellboy, and Chef Sussman. Janice from the boutique had to hang up. She's got a customer. Everybody ready? You're all on with Mr. Speer."

Amy nestled up close to Mike and shared the receiver. Since she had started this whole thing, she felt honor-bound to listen.

"Hi, Mr. Speer? This is Bobby Marrin. I'll start things off."

Amy had already started to giggle. Mike knew exactly what she was thinking. A joke told by four people was like a horse created by a committee. It couldn't help but turn out to be a camel.

"A man goes into a pet store to buy an unusual pet. The clerk points to—"

"Wait a second, Bobby," Fred chimed in. "You forgot to say the man was married."

"Oh, yeah. A married man goes into a pet store to buy—"

"Hold it!" Chef Sussman interrupted. "You've got to add that the man is henpecked."

Alice broke into the conversation. "Henpecked is a sexist term, Chef Sussman. Can't you think of another word?"

"I only know one other word. It's puss—"

"That's enough!" Alice sounded frantic. "You can say henpecked, I guess."

Bobby Marrin came back on the line. "Okay, a henpecked married man goes into a pet store to—"

"Wait, Bobby!" Stan Chassler's voice cut in. "I don't think it was a pet store. I heard the henpecked married man went to a zoo. That's where he found the Crunch-Bird."

"They don't sell animals at zoos, Stan. They sell them in pet stores."

"Well . . . okay. I guess it doesn't make any difference."

"I'll start again." Bobby sounded weary. "A henpecked married man goes into a pet store to—"

"Stan could be right." Alice broke in. "They *do* sell animals at the zoo. My cousin in San Diego adopted a skink, whatever that is."

"It's a lizard," Fred informed her. "It's common in many regions of the Old and New World. It has flat, smooth, overlapping scales and—"

"Enough already!" Alice sounded shocked. "I was hoping it was something sweet and cuddly."

Chef Sussman came on the line. "I used to live in California, Alice, and I know about zoo adoptions. You don't actually take the animals home with you. You pay the adoption fee and your name goes on a plaque outside the exhibit. It's a way of supporting the zoo. Go ahead, Bobby, tell the joke. I've got meringues in the oven."

"All right, here we go. A married man goes into a pet store—"

"A *henpecked* married man!"

"Okay. A *henpecked* married man goes . . ."

Mike took the receiver and put it under the pillow. Then he put his finger to his lips and pulled Amy out of bed, leading her from the room.

"Get dressed. Wear anything. We're leaving here in two minutes."

"But, Mike—"

"Don't argue. Just get dressed. Now!"

Two minutes later Mike and Amy got off at the main floor where Mike ushered Amy out the door, into a waiting taxi. "The airport. And hurry."

The taxi pulled out and Amy turned to Mike in amazement. "Where are we going?"

"Las Vegas. We can get married there, right away."

Amy's mouth opened and shut. She wasn't about to argue with a suggestion like that.

"Can I ask why?"

"Sure. I decided you were right. Somebody up there's protecting your virtue. If we get married, maybe we'll actually get the chance to sleep together without being interrupted."

Amy laughed. "I wish I'd brought my special pillow. I've never slept without it."

"You don't need a special pillow for tonight. You've got me."

Amy smiled as Mike hugged her. He was right. Katy

could sleep on her pillow tonight. "What about the Crunch-Bird? You missed your only chance to hear that joke."

"Crunch-Bird?" The driver spoke up. "I know that one. You wanna hear it?"

"Why not?" Mike pulled Amy into his arms in the darkness of the back seat.

"A henpecked little man walks into a pet store. He wants an unusual gift for his wife's birthday.

" 'Sure, I got something unusual,' the clerk tells him. 'It's a Crunch-Bird. He's been trained, but you gotta be real careful about giving the commands. Watch this.'

"The clerk takes an ordinary-looking bird out of its cage and sets it on a perch. He holds up an empty pop can.

" 'Crunch-Bird, the pop can!'

"The bird flies off the perch, grabs the pop can, and crunches it in his powerful beak.

" 'Wow! That's great!' The henpecked little man is impressed. 'Let me try it.'

"He takes out a package of cigarettes and holds it up.

" 'Crunch-Bird, my cigarettes.'

"The bird makes a dive for the cigarettes and crunches them in his beak.

" 'I'll take him,' the little man says. 'My wife's gonna love this bird.'

"Five minutes later the man gets home with his Crunch-Bird. His wife is sitting on the couch, drinking a martini.

" 'I bought you a little present today, sweetheart,' he says. He takes the bird out of the cage and sets it on its perch.

" 'A bird?' The wife isn't happy. 'You're an idiot, George. You know I hate birds.'

" 'But this one's special, sweetheart. It's been specially trained as a Crunch-Bird.'

" 'Crunch-Bird?' His wife gives a nasty laugh. 'Crunch-Bird, my ass!'

There was a long moment of silence. The taxi driver waited but his passengers didn't laugh. That was strange. This joke usually had them rolling in the aisles.

"Don't you get it? Crunch-Bird, my *ass.*"

There was total silence from the backseat. The driver looked in the mirror and started to grin. Love. It made you deaf, dumb, and blind. They were locked in a kiss back there and neither one of them had heard a word he'd said.